THE
ECONOMICS
OF
IMMIGRATION

Allocating Life, Liberty

and the Pursuit of Happiness

REVISED FIRST EDITION

DAVID BERNOTAS

University of California, San Diego

San Diego, CA

Bassim Hamadeh, Publisher
Michael Simpson, Vice President of Acquisitions
Christopher Foster, Vice President of Marketing
Jessica Knott, Managing Editor
Stephen Milano, Creative Director
Kevin Fahey, Cognella Marketing Program Manager
Seidy Cruz Hamadeh, Acquisitions Editor
Erin Escobar, Licensing Associate

First published in the United States of America in 2012 by University Readers, Inc.

15 14 13 12 11   1 2 3 4 5

Printed in the United States of America

ISBN: 978-1-62131-001-3

www.cognella.com 800.200.3908

Contents

Background

This book was developed as a supplement for a course at UCSD. As such, it was designed to be used in a 10-week, low-level elective. The prerequisite for this material is an introductory economics course. No knowledge of econometrics or regression theory is assumed, and nearly all mathematical detail will be swept under the rug.

Recent research on this topic is abundant. Obviously, as policies and data sources evolve, this stock of literature will continue to grow. Most of what appears here is not original work. Other related readings (and sources from which much of this material was taken) include pieces by George Borjas and Gordon Hanson, among others. Ultimately, it is my goal to have this text become a basic and self-contained overview of the issues and details concerning the economics of immigration in the United States. I have no illusions of significantly contributing to ongoing research—this manuscript is intentionally designed to be an overview of existing literature. I will leave the frontier research to the experts.

One of the biggest challenges I face teaching a course on the economics of immigration is unifying an audience with diverse backgrounds. Since the topic attracts economists, sociologists, political scientists, students of international relations, and so on, I face the hurdle of teaching some students with strong opinions supported by weak training. To address this, the first part of this book gives a bare-bones overview of some of the relevant economic theory and tools we will need to master in order to read and understand empirical papers on this subject.

Unavoidably, I find that one of the biggest ideas students take from this course is whether immigration is good or bad. This decision is made important by the seemingly endless debate about immigration—from Arizona's most recent laws to immigrants' consumption of welfare and social services—I think far too many people are taking part in an argument that they know little or nothing about. Much like other political issues, immigration is ultimately a debate about how to divide the economic pie—it is an issue of allocation. It would be very surprising if denying immigrants everything (including admission) is optimal for a country's natives. Likewise, trying to develop a worldwide welfare state funded by native tax-payers is also unlikely to be the best policy. Thus, we need to discuss degrees of allocation, and evaluate how those degrees affect natives and immigrants in both the short run and long run. In doing so, we will cross the bridge over several key issues:

1. Why migrate? This may seem like an unnecessary question to ask, particularly for students residing in the United States given the abundant immigrant population, but the motives behind relocating (particularly across borders) must be explored. We will also briefly examine how the immigration process works and how policy has changed since its inception.

2. Who migrates? This involves discussion of the skills of immigrants, where these people are coming from, and how these factors have evolved over time. This question interestingly seems to be more at the heart of the (uninformed) immigration debate than the others listed here, I think primarily out of bigotry. The general idea that immigrants are "different" from us is sufficient reason to keep them out, according to many. However, as we will see, these differences are solely and entirely responsible for any benefit gained by natives from immigration—which makes immigration a bitter (but beneficial!) pill for some natives to swallow.

3. How do immigrants affect natives? This is the bulk of the material, and the bulk of the importance of this issue. Immigrants affect wages, and thus affect the welfare of native workers and consumers. However, the details of how they affect native welfare are less than straight-forward. In addition, immigrants promote movement of native workers and firms within the country, which changes how the economy looks over time. There is also the issue of external benefits and costs to immigration— immigration brings good things like delicious cuisine and cultural diversity, but it also brings bad things like disgusting cuisine, weird accents, and bad drivers. I'm intentionally being abrasive here to make a point—what constitutes an external benefit or cost may ultimately turn out to be a matter of opinion—and opinions are frequently uneducated.

4. How much welfare and how many public goods are consumed by immigrants? This boils down to the question of "do immigrants pay their way?" Immigrants do in fact consume public aid. This entails a transfer from natives to immigrants, which most people view as a bad thing. (Don't forget, there are also transfers from immigrants to natives too ... and from immigrants to immigrants!) This too is a hot topic of debate. For our purposes, the punch line is that a slightly higher percentage of immigrants consume public assistance than their native counterparts, but there are *far* fewer immigrants than natives—so the total amount of aid consumed is greater for natives than immigrants.

5. How should immigration policy be made? When I first started teaching economics, I used a textbook written by Greg Mankiw that makes a point in an early chapter of emphasizing a fundamental tradeoff in economics: fairness versus efficiency. You can't have both. This tradeoff is everywhere in immigration policy—who should be allowed to come, who should we keep out? Should only the rich be given permission to enter

the United States? (Should we sell citizenship?) I'm sure for many of you, when you read these types of questions, your immediate reaction (partly because you're young) is "No! Allowing only the rich to become citizens is not fair!" This may be especially true if you weigh the health and safety benefits of living in the United States. Immigrating here may in fact save somebody's life, or keep a child from starving—certainly we can't reserve this benefit to only the wealthy! But we can, and we do. We sell food, we sell medicine, and we sell all kinds of other things that could benefit the poor (like education)—in essence we reserve the benefit of these goods to the wealthy. So why should immigration be different? Maybe it shouldn't be.

You may ultimately take with you something from this course that is not among the categories listed above, and that's fine. However, I hope you'll think twice about anything listed here that you think isn't an important issue in immigration, because you may be off track.

During the time it took me to put this text together, a plethora of articles appeared in the newspaper concerning immigration. I read the *Wall Street Journal* and clipped many of these articles and included them here to give you a sense of relevancy. Unlike many topics in economics, I think immigration is one of the easiest-to-find real-world applications, but I still offer these articles as proof that what we do here is not irrelevant to the people living around us.

Chapter 1

Economics 101

What follows is designed to be a reference for those of you with holes in your economics training. It obviously is too brief to substitute for an introductory course, but it may help some of you get over the hump of understanding key concepts that will be presented in later chapters.

Supply/Demand

If you were to stop a random passerby on the street and ask them what they know about economics, their answer would undoubtedly include the words "supply" and "demand." Unfortunately, since these two words are easy to say, people say them often—too often, probably. Although we can in fact show a surprisingly large amount of interesting economic concepts using simple supply/demand diagrams, "supply and demand" is not the cause for and solution to everything economic.[1] However, no economist can dismiss the importance of supply and demand as a fundamental concept, and it would thus be unwise to proceed without a little review.

The Demand Curve

One of the greatest inventions in economics was the ability to represent a person's preferences—gooey, warm and fuzzy, non-quantifiable masses of emotional likes and dislikes—as mathematical functions.[2] If a person's preferences satisfy just a couple simple conditions[3], then we can represent those preferences via a nice (maybe even differentiable) utility function.[4] Once we have a utility function, we can employ the

---

[1] I personally think that opportunity cost should take the trump card for the single most important topic in an introductory economics course ... but for some reason, it lacks the sex appeal of supply and demand in the eyes of the non-economist.

[2] Thank you Leon Walras (1834–1920).

[3] E.g.: completeness, transitivity, reflexivity.

[4] Although beyond the reach of most readers, the text by Mas-Collel, Whinston and Green is, in my opinion, the bible on consumer theory. Hal Varian's "Intermediate Microeconomics" text, which is designed for undergraduates, is an accessible substitute.

Figure 1.1

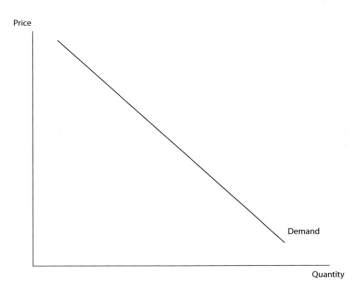

well-understood tools of calculus[5] to derive conclusions about how consumers will behave.

One of these conclusions is the demand function. It is the result of consumers trying their best to maximize their happiness—maximize their utility—given the limitations of their income and prices they face in the marketplace. One result of the utility maximization problem is this: as price of a good goes up, consumers tend to buy less of the good. This is frequently referred to as the law of demand. *Thus, demand curves are downward sloping.*

Note that demand curves do not have to be linear, although we tend to draw them this way for simplicity. Also note that the axis labels on these diagrams are illogical—consumers typically see the price of a good, then decide how much to buy, so that price determines quantity demanded—but we draw it backwards so that it appears that quantity determines price. This is just an old habit economists have, much to the dismay of mathematicians (who certainly mock economists when behind closed doors).

Demand curves are essentially a graphical representation of how consumers value a good. Specifically, if you pick the quantity of the good, the height of the demand curve tells us how much consumers value that unit of the good. So, the height of the demand curve above Q=100 tells us how valuable the 100th unit is.

---

[5] Thank you Isaac Newton (1643–1727).

Changes in Demand

Since the demand curve is a graphical result of consumers' maximizing their utility subject to their budget constraints, it follows that any changes to the utility function or to the budget constraint will result in changes to the demand curve. Specifically, changes in preferences, expectations, income, prices of other goods, et cetera, will result in a shift of the demand curve. Upward shifts of the demand curve reflect an increase in the value of the good.[6] Typical changes that result in an upward shift of demand: an increase in income (if the good is normal), a decrease in the price of a complement, an increase in the price of a substitute, or a change in preferences or expectations that make the good more desirable.

It is vital that you do not confuse a shift of the demand curve with movement along the demand curve. A shift is caused by a change in one of the factors mentioned above: income, preferences, and so on. If the demand curve shifts up, then it is safe to say that at any price, more is demanded. (You may wish to prove this to yourself graphically.) This is in contrast to the movement from one point to another along the same demand curve, which means that price of the good in question has changed—but income, preferences, and everything else has stayed the same. If price falls, then it is in fact true that more of that good will be demanded, but this movement is very different from a shift of the demand curve. For this reason, statements like "demand goes up" are sloppy and dangerous because this statement does not make clear what is going on.

Elasticity

"Change in demand" refers to a shift of the curve resulting from a change in one or several of the factors discussed above. One factor that does not make the list of things that will shift a demand: changes in price. Changes in price will not shift the demand curve. A change in price will move us from one point on the demand curve (associated with price p_1 in Figure 1.2) to another point on the same demand curve (associated with price p_2).

Elasticity is a tool that measures how sensitive quantity is to these changes in price. Elasticity has no units—it is a scale ranging from zero (quantity is completely unresponsive to price changes) to $-\infty$ (quantity is infinitely responsive to price changes). The negative sign is important since price and quantity move in opposite directions! Also please keep in mind that elasticity is not the same as slope—slope has units of

---

[6] It would be correct to call an upward shift a "shift to the right" instead, but some of the interpretation would be lost. Remember, the height of the demand curve represents the value of the good to consumers. If the demand curve shifts up, then the height of the demand curve has increased, and so we conclude that value of the good has also increased. If I say the demand shifted to the right, then the focus on the height of the curve is lost in exchange for a focus that is on the quantity instead of price.

Figure 1.2

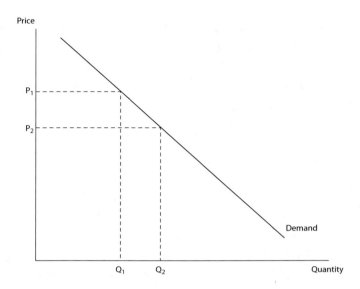

price/quantity—elasticity has no units. True, the two concepts of slope and elasticity are related, but they are not the same.

The general formula for elasticity of demand is $\frac{\% \Delta Q}{\% \Delta P}$. Some baby math gives us the following decomposition:

$$\frac{\% \Delta Q}{\% \Delta P} = \frac{\Delta Q/Q}{\Delta P/P} = \frac{\Delta Q}{\Delta P} \frac{P}{Q} = \frac{1}{slope} \frac{P}{Q} .$$

There are a few things to notice at this point. The first is that all of these expressions are negative since price and quantity move in opposite directions. The second is that, since the slope of the demand curve appears in the denominator of the last expression, there is an inverse relationship between slope and elasticity—as the slope becomes more negative (demand curve gets steeper), elasticity becomes less negative (i.e., closer to zero). Likewise, as the slope becomes less negative (flatter demand curve), elasticity becomes more negative and approaches -∞. Somewhere in the middle of this range is the special value of -1, or "unit elastic" demand. Elasticity numbers closer to zero are called "inelastic" (demand is less sensitive to price changes), and numbers farther from zero are called "elastic" (demand is more sensitive to price changes).

There are some interesting connections between elasticity and the areas we will eventually identify beneath the demand curve. Particularly, areas of consumer surplus, total revenue, and dead-weight loss are all affected via policies in ways that involve consideration of elasticity of the demand curve.

The Supply Curve

If we shift our focus from consumers to producers, we move from a discussion of maximizing utility subject to budget constraints to one of minimizing cost subject to output or technology constraints of production.[7] From the solution of this cost minimization problem comes the supply curve. Similar to our discussion of demand, the height of the supply curve at Q=100 represents the cost of producing the 100th unit of the good. It seems logical that as a firm produces more and more of a good, the resources it uses in production will become scarce. Thus, as quantity increases, the firm will demand higher and higher prices for each good, reflecting the increasingly scarce (and thus increasingly expensive) inputs. For this reason, *supply curves are upward sloping.*

Shifts in the supply curve are caused by things that change the cost of production: typically changes in the price of inputs or resources, changes in technology, and a change in the number of firms. The concept of elasticity of supply is relevant, and follows the same intuitive details as for elasticity of demand.

Consumer Surplus, Producer Surplus, and Efficiency

The interaction between supply and demand is in fact a bit magical. Consumers—completely self-involved, thinking of no one but themselves—maximizing their happiness, and firms—thinking only of the bottom line—minimizing production cost in order to keep profits as large as possible, interacting without instruction, to produce one of the best-oiled machines in the world: the market economy.[8]

Before you dig in and launch a socialist campaign against my last statement, realize this: despite the nearly flawless nature of the market economy, there is frequently a need for government. Government facilitates transfers, prevents free-riders, provides public goods, addresses issues of fairness, and can even correct some market failure. However, the government is a big, planned-out, deliberate institution that struggles at times to even make ends meet. A market economy, on the other hand, naturally emerges from our self-centered desires to be happy. And the market works. You have to appreciate something so simple and untainted. It's like the difference between natural beauty and cosmetic surgery—although they both may get the job done, only one is a gift from God. (Now you can launch your campaign....)

---

[7] Minimizing costs and maximizing profits will result in the same production decisions within the firm.

[8] I'm sure most of you don't have a problem with my claim about firms' pursuit of profit, but many of you may retch at the idea of selfish consumers since you yourself are a consumer. You are selfish. Everything you do or buy is done or bought to help one person—you. Even gifts to charity fit this bill, since the happiness you derive from a donation must outweigh the loss you feel from having less money. So you donate because it increases your utility—a very selfish move (that coincidentally helps other people).

To illustrate the power of the market economy, we need to talk about efficiency. As it turns out, in most cases, nothing is more efficient than a market economy. As will be clear shortly, the way we define efficiency ignores all concepts of fairness. *Efficiency is the idea that we want the economic pie to be as large as possible.* We don't care who gets a big slice and who gets a small slice, as long as the pie is as big as can be. You may see obvious problems with this, but for now just note: there is a tradeoff between efficiency and fairness. If your primary concern is fairness—making sure that everybody gets an equal slice of the pie—that's ok. Just realize that somebody else may think efficiency—the size of the pie—is more important and the two of you will probably never be friends! It's a version of the saying "you can't have your cake and eat it too," but now it's "you can't maximize efficiency and maximize fairness too."

The intuition behind this seemingly brutal statement isn't complicated. Think of a building on your college campus that is named after a person. There's a good chance that building was named after them because they gave tons of money to either build or renovate the place. In other words, they're rich. Having rich people is efficient—it results in buildings being built—that's a big pie! How would things be different if we took some of their money away and gave it to the poor? Well, chances are they wouldn't be rich enough to donate money, so the building wouldn't be named after them. What's more, if we took money from all rich people, nobody would be rich enough to donate and the building would never even be built. That's a smaller pie. So, we have fairness on one hand, efficiency on the other. Increasing one means decreasing the other (usually).

How do we measure efficiency? Consider this: for any market price resulting in a certain number of units being consumed, at least one person would have been willing to pay a little more for the good than they had to. The difference between what you are willing to pay and what you have to pay is called consumer surplus (CS). If I am willing to pay $10, but the price was $8, I get $2 worth of consumer surplus. The more surplus I receive, the better off I am. Adding up the CS for all consumers in a market gives us a dollar value that approximates the well-being of consumers. Likewise, it is safe to say that for any market price where some units were sold, some firm out there would have been willing to take a slightly lower price for the good. The difference between the amount of money that a firm is willing to accept and the amount they actually get is called producer surplus (PS), and the sum of all PS across firms gives us a dollar value approximating welfare of firms.

Finding these areas in a supply and demand diagram is simple. CS is the area above price and below the demand curve. PS is the area below price and above the supply curve. These two areas are bound on the left by the y-axis and on the right by the quantity exchanged Q*.

If we ignore institutions like the government, we can divide everybody into one of two groups: consumers and producers. This means that everybody in the economy

Figure 1.3

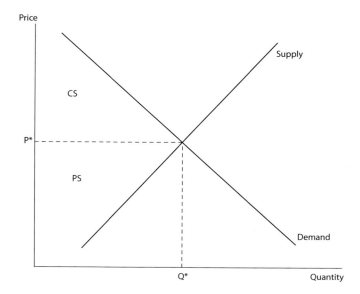

collects either CS or PS. Thus, the sum of CS + PS measures the welfare of society as a whole. As a benevolent leader, one might be interested in developing policies that maximize this sum—and thus maximize the welfare of society. This is our definition of efficiency: *a policy is efficient if it maximizes the sum of CS + PS.*

Here is a critical fact to note: if the government were developing a policy to determine what price to charge for a good, and it wanted to maximize social welfare (i.e., it wanted the policy to be efficient), it would pick a price of P* for the good—exactly the same price that the market chooses if left alone! Thus, the outcome of a market economy that has not been tampered with is the best possible outcome from society's point of view. The market maximizes social welfare—it is efficient all by itself.

Some Inefficient Policies

Let's consider some government policies that are not efficient, i.e., these policies do not maximize CS + PS. This inefficiency is not by design, nor is it due to government ignorance. We know these policies result in a loss of social welfare, and we implement them anyway. Why? Just as I mentioned before, sometimes we are willing to sacrifice efficiency in order to gain fairness. So these policies should be fairer than the market outcome of letting supply equal demand. The question is this: to whom is the policy fair? The unfortunate answer sometimes is that the policy is fair to the group that lobbies or supports the government decision makers the most. So, unfortunately for most, it's possible that the government implements a policy that is "fair" to oil companies or "fair" to people who abuse the system.

Price controls are the simplest example of policies that are inefficient. One group (either producers or consumers) convinces the government that the market price of P* is unfair for them. In response to this persuasion, the government will pass a law restricting price—either price must stay above a certain level if we want to help firms (price floor), or price must stay below a certain level if we want to help consumers (price ceiling). Examples are rent control and a minimum wage.

The impact of these policies on social welfare is clear from a simple supply and demand diagram in Figure 1.4 (in this case, the diagram is for a price floor). Since the price control by definition changes the price of the good, the quantity exchanged must also change. Specifically, Q will fall to whichever is smaller, supply or demand, at the chosen price. As a result, new areas of consumer and producer surplus must be found, with the addition of a new triangular region called dead-weight loss (DWL). Notice that for all P ≠ P*, CS + PS is smaller than before. This is clear since the area DWL used to be part of the sum CS + PS, and now it is not.

Where does DWL go? It goes nowhere. It is literally potential happiness that could be captured by consumers and producers, but isn't. What causes DWL? It is simply the result of producing the wrong amount of the good. In order to make society as happy

Figure 1.4

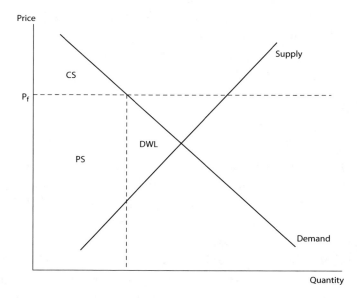

as possible, we should produce where the supply curve intersects the demand curve. We're not doing so in this diagram thanks to the price control. In general, any policy that results in the wrong amount of the good being exchanged (from society's point of view) will result in DWL.

Does the existence of DWL mean we should eliminate this policy? No. Remember the original goal of this price control was to help producers (in this case, since it's a price floor). Did we accomplish this? Yes, we probably did. To determine if we were successful in helping producers, we need to compare the size of PS after the policy with PS before the policy. If the area has increased, we were successful in increasing the welfare of firms. Won't the new PS always be bigger? Nope. It's possible, depending on the elasticity of the supply and demand curves, to draw a price floor where firms are worse off after the policy. That would be a horrible policy—both consumers and producers would be worse off after the price control. If this were the case, we really screwed up and should consider removing the price floor since nobody will support its existence.

Other policies that result in DWL (and therefore are not efficient) include things like taxes and barriers to trade. Please keep in mind, although all of these policies result in some lost social welfare, they may still be serving a purpose—the improvement in welfare of a particular, chosen group within society. This discussion will obviously be revisited when we talk about immigration policy, since we will be concerned with how policies affect society and groups within like natives or immigrants.

Regression Overview

The majority of work in the field of immigration and the economics of immigration is empirical work. Essentially people scouring the Earth for data to figure out one thing or another about how immigration works, how it affects us, and what immigrants look like. This being the case, a student of immigration economics must have at least a basic understanding of econometrics and regression theory. We have the luxury of foregoing the background in probability theory (don't underestimate the importance of probability theory!) since our primary focus is simply to learn how to interpret empirical results. Ultimately, you need to be able to read published articles on this subject and understand what they are saying.

The program we use to handle data sets is called STATA. There are obviously substitutes like SAS, Eviews, and so on. All of these programs will be similar for our purposes, although the cosmetics may be slightly different.

One critical thing to know about economics is this: we employ the scientific model. As such, the first step in an empirical project involves figuring out what question you want to answer and then turning immediately to economic theory. Do not skip the theory. Many young researchers want to whack away at a question with data and see what kind of results they get, then they work backwards and try to figure out why they saw what they saw. If price goes up, and you find in response that quantity demanded also goes up, this should be a red flag! If you skipped the theory part of the process, you may not see problems as obvious as this. Force yourself to follow this recipe:

1. Develop the question or model
2. Determine what economic theory says about the issue
3. Collect data
4. Run regressions
5. Evaluate and conclude

The term "regression" refers to a generally straight-forward technique of fitting a line to a scatter plot of data points. Obviously we want the line to "fit" the data as well as possible. The particular way this is done gets complicated (sort of), but it can be summarized as this: position the line over the scatter plot so that the distance from the line to all of the points is as small as possible. If you move the line upward to shrink the distance to points above the line, then you are simultaneously increasing the distance to points below the line. This give and take is what determines the unique best position for the line to be placed. Once positioned, we can make inferences about the slope of that line and in turn draw conclusions about the relationship between the x-variable and the y-variable. This is obviously an overgeneralization, and there are details both large and small that I am intentionally ignoring, but this should at least give you a mental image of what goes on when you tell STATA to run a regression.

Let's do a simple example. Step 1 is to develop a model or a question. So, let's try to estimate or predict how much beer a person drinks. What factors contribute to beer consumption? The price of beer and a person's income certain play a part in determining how much a person consumes. With this in mind, I propose the following model:

$$BEER = \beta_0 + \beta_1 PRICE + \beta_2 INCOME + u$$

where BEER is the amount of beer consumed annually in ounces, PRICE is the price of beer in dollars and INCOME is a person's income in dollars. There may be a very good argument to include other variables, but let's keep it simple for now. Notice that this equation is very similar to the equation for a line (technically it's a plane) $y = mx + b$. The y is replaced with BEER (the dependent variable), m is replaced with β_1 and β_2, x is replaced with PRICE and INCOME, and b is replaced with β_0. So this is the equation for the line that we will try to fit to our scatter plot. The u in the equation above is the error term; it must be present for technical reasons if you want to go to economics heaven.

We now turn to step 2 on the recipe: determine what economic theory says about the issue. I know you probably had to use this part of your brain a little for #1 on the recipe too, since figuring out what variables to include is kind of an economic-theory thought process. However, I want you to consciously think some more about theory in the context of our model. What should the signs of the coefficients β_1 and β_2 be? As PRICE goes up, what happens to the variable BEER? Do they move in the same direction? If so, β_1 should be positive. What does economic theory say? (Think: law of demand.) Price and quantity move in opposite directions, so β_1 should be negative. As INCOME goes up, what happens to BEER? It goes up too, so β_2 should be positive.[9] We must predict the signs of our coefficients before we run the regression. It keeps us honest.

Now on to step 3 of the recipe: collect data. So hit the books, internet, streets; make surveys; and so on until you think you have all the data you need.[10] Collecting data is the hard part. The data you find will almost always be terrible—you'll be missing data, you won't find the data you want, you won't find the years that you want, et cetera. Don't worry. You can almost always make do. For our beer consumption model, suppose you have data on personal beer consumption and income, as well as data on beer prices.

Step 4: regress. Plug all of your hard-earned data into STATA and type the magic command "regress." (This text will not teach you how to use the program STATA, our goal is to learn how to understand what the program spits out.) The following will appear:

Reg Beer Price Income

Source	SS	df	MS		Number of obs	=	41
					F(2, 38)	=	60.86
Model	160436327	2	80218163.5		Prob > F	=	0.0000
Residual	50089039.3	38	1318132.61		R-squared	=	0.7621
					Adj R-squared	=	0.7496
Total	210525366	40	5263134.16		Root MSE	=	1148.1

beer	Coef.	Std. Err.	t	P > |t|	[95% conf. interval]	
Price	3.364986	1.127409	2.98	0.005	1.082665	5.647306
income	1680191	456709.9	3.68	0.001	755630.5	2604752
_cons	−7563.611	4449.871	−1.70	0.097	−16571.9	1444.683

This is a typical example of regression output. We won't use every bit of information presented in these tables (although I assure you that everything presented has some purpose). We will primarily be interested in the lower table, particularly the columns labeled "Coef." and "P>|t|." Notice that the left-most column of the lower table is the

---

[9] You might be able to structure a viable theoretically supported argument that as income goes up, beer consumption goes down. Maybe rich people drink only wine. If this is what theory tells you, then go with it. Theory (and personal experience) tells me that more income leads to more beer.

[10] For the record: "data" is plural, "datum" is singular. So you say "These data are…" not "This data is…."

variable names, where "_cons" is short for "constant" which is nothing more than the y-intercept (β_0) for the line that we have now fit to our scatter plot. We will almost never worry about the intercept.

The column labeled "Coef." is all of the slopes like β_1 and β_2. The interpretation of this column goes something like this: if the price of beer goes up by one unit (which, in this case, would be one dollar) then a person's beer consumption goes up by 3.3649 units (here, 3.3649 ounces). Likewise, if a person's income increases by one unit (here, the units are dollars), then their beer consumption will go up by 1,680,191 units.

The columns labeled "Std.Err." "t" and "P>|t|" tell us how confident we can be in our results. More precisely, it tells us the chance that the slope we estimated (i.e., 3.3649) is actually zero. To be confident that your result is significantly different from zero, look for small standard errors, big t-statistics, and small P>|t|. It's probably easiest to reference the P>|t| column, since the other two require some familiarity with probability theory (or the tables in your statistics book) to understand. So, for the slope coefficient on PRICE, there is only a 0.5% chance (0.005) that our result was pure luck and the slope is actually zero instead of 3.36. Obviously, the closer to zero the values in this column are, the more confident we can be in our results.

Here is a recipe for interpreting regression output:

1. Look at the sign of the coefficient—is it consistent with what your theory predicted?
2. Look at the magnitude of the coefficient—does it make sense?
3. Look at the significance of the coefficient—can you trust your estimate?

So how would we use this recipe to interpret our results above? Well, looking at the signs of the coefficients, we see that both PRICE and INCOME have positive slope coefficients. Is this consistent with what our theory predicts? No. The price of beer and the amount of beer consumed should move in opposite directions—so if PRICE goes up, BEER should fall—the slope should be negative. The sign of the coefficient for INCOME requires a little more thought. We see a positive sign, implying that as income goes up, so too will beer consumption. That seems plausible—this means that beer is a normal good. Is that what theory predicts? Maybe, but maybe not. (This is why you must visit your theory *first*!) I am not entirely sure beer is a normal good. In fact, I think some empirical evidence may imply that beer is an inferior good, and as people earn more money, they move to more expensive alternatives like wine and brandy. However, the positive value for the INCOME coefficient isn't offensive like the positive sign for PRICE.

So the sign of the PRICE coefficient is wrong, while the sign of the INCOME coefficient is fine as long as you're ok with beer being a normal good. What about the magnitudes? Does the fact that a one-dollar increase in the price of beer causes a 3-ounce change in consumption make sense? Remember, BEER measures the annual consumption of beer. I would think a 3-ounce change is fairly small in light of a one-dollar jump in price, but the value isn't totally ridiculous. The coefficient for INCOME on the other hand is absurd. If a person makes one more dollar, they will increase their annual consumption of beer by nearly 1.7 million ounces! That's an increase of about 140,000 bottles of beer per year in light of a one-dollar raise. This makes no sense.

Are the estimates significant? Yes. Both the PRICE and INCOME coefficients have very small p-values of 0.005 and 0.001 respectively. This means we should have considerable confidence in our estimates (despite the above-mentioned problems). Typically, a researcher would like better than 10% or maybe 5% significance, which is equivalent to a p-value of 0.10 or 0.05.

For the most part, the papers and publications relevant to immigration economics will be trying to determine if variable A affects variable B, and if so, how. In other words, most of the literature we will see is simply trying to estimate the value of the coefficient for a single variable. True, most models (like the one above) will have several variables, but the coefficients for most of them will be well understood prior to the writing of the paper. For example, it is well understood how price affects beer consumption. Thus, if we were to write a paper using the model above, we would most likely be testing the hypothesis that beer is normal—so we are focusing on the coefficient for a single variable (income). As it turns out, our results support the idea that beer is normal. This is how the thought process should work for the majority of empirical literature.

Some of the literature in this field is beyond the level of comfort for undergraduates. However, even if the paper is very advanced, it is likely that at some point they present regression results that look strikingly similar to those above. Thus, it is safe to say that, despite the difficulty of the paper, you will be able to get a general idea as to what they are finding.

Trade Overview

It seems logical that immigration and trade would have some significant overlap. Both deal with things (goods or people) coming from other countries and the subsequent welfare impact of this movement. In fact, one can easily extend this logic and say that a country faces two options: import a television from country A or import the people from country A who make the television. Although these two options are obviously not exactly the same, and will thus have varied economic impact on the destination country, it is safe to say that immigration and trade can be viewed as gross substitutes for each other.

With this in mind, a brief review of trade is in order. One theme will result: trade makes everybody better off. Now, one has to be diligent to remember that we are talking about the size of the economic pie, not who gets a big slice. Perhaps I should restate my claim: trade makes all pies bigger. Division of these pies may still be an issue for some.

There are two obvious choices a country faces when dealing with trade: export or import. Which to choose is simple. If the prevailing world price for the good is higher than the domestic price, you should export the good. If the prevailing world price is lower than the domestic price, then import the good. The corresponding diagrams are shown in Figures 1.5 and 1.6.

Clearly, in either case, the combined area of CS + PS is bigger than it would be for the case of no trade where only domestic supply and domestic demand exist. In the case of exports, producers add a bit of surplus to PS, and in the case of imports, consumers are made better off by way of additional CS. Notice too that, in addition to the new area of PS or CS, there is a transfer from one group to the other. In the case of exports, for example, some CS is transferred to producers. Thus, although society is better off thanks to the larger CS + PS, either group may have reason to complain about free trade.

So how do we satisfy the complaints about trade? First of all, please note that any complaint about free trade is likely not based on economic reason. The economist view on trade is simple: trade makes everybody better off. However, for reasons not economic, we do find that there are cases in which restricting trade can silence some complaining (or lobbying) from certain groups. Although there are several tools available to us, we focus primarily on two of the most simple: tariffs and quotas. A tariff is simply a unit tax on imports. For each car you want to send to the United States, you must pay a $100 per unit tax. A quota is a limit on the number of imports. You can send cars to the United States for free, but only a certain number. Beyond that number, no cars will be allowed.

Figures 1.5 and 1.6

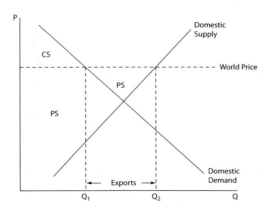
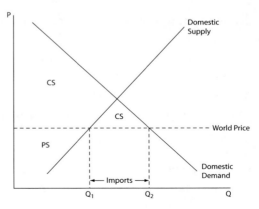

Figure 1.7

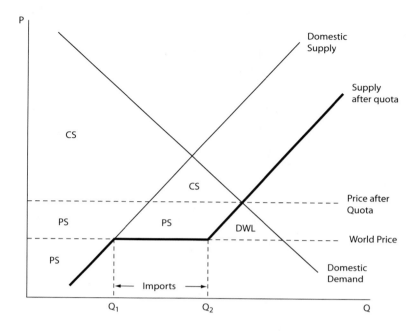

Figure 1.8

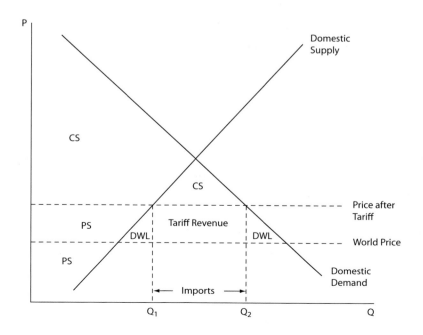

Since both policies result in a change in the number of good exchanged, we can expect to find some dead-weight loss. The source of this DWL can be viewed as inefficient domestic producers—firms that had production costs too high to compete with international producers—that are now able to stay in business. Also notice in Figures 1.7 and 1.8 that either of the two policies succeeds in increasing the size of producer surplus, primarily at the expense of consumers. One final note about PS: the parallelogram labeled "PS" that is above the word "imports" goes to foreign producers in the case of a quota. This area is exactly the same size as the tariff revenue in the right diagram, which goes to the government.

Since the number of imports, the price of the good, and the size of CS, PS, and DWL are all the same in the two diagrams, domestic producers and consumers are indifferent between these two policies. Both result in the same thing: domestic firms are better off, consumers are worse off, and society suffers due to the inefficiency introduced by domestic producers. These outcomes make either policy seem ridiculous, but remember what our goal was—to please firms. We were not trying to increase the size of the pie.

Labor Markets

The area of economics with which immigration issues overlap most is probably labor economics. The good news for us is that labor economics is a very well-studied, well-understood area of economics, so we have plenty of good theory to recycle.

In a labor market, workers are the suppliers. They offer themselves or their time to firms, who are the demanders. *You do not demand a job, you supply your time.* Thus, the appropriate interpretation of the height of the supply curve for a labor market is the wage required for you to show up to work (i.e., it's the cost or reservation wage of the last worker hired). The height of the demand curve is interpreted as the value of the last worker hired. The demand curve is downward sloping because the first worker is more productive than the last (or you could say that your first hour of work is more productive than your last). This is the property of diminishing marginal product of labor (MP_L). You have experienced diminishing MP_L in your own life—when you study, and your productivity falls as you get tired.

If we assume that workers are paid what they're worth, then the height of the demand curve represents how much the firm is willing to pay a worker. Determining the value of a worker is straight-forward. We measure output before we hire you, then measure output again after we hire you. The difference is the number of goods you contributed—your marginal product of labor. Multiply this number by the price of whatever it is you're producing and we have your value—your marginal revenue

Figure 1.9

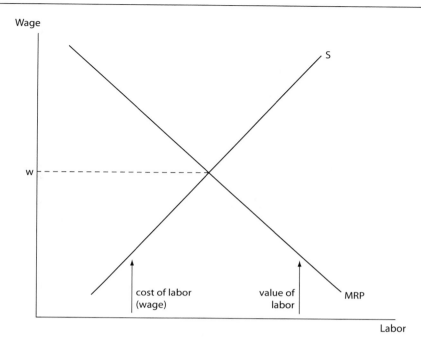

product (MRP).[11] With this in mind, we tend to label the demand curve with "marginal revenue product" or "MRP" instead of "D" for labor market discussions.

Things that improve productivity of labor, such as technological advancements or investment in capital (human or physical) will shift the MRP curve upward. The interpretation is that firms are now willing to pay more for each worker since they are each more productive than before. Things that increase the number of workers will shift the supply curve to the right, so that at any given wage rate, more workers are willing to work. For example, when college tuition increases relative to the price of other things in the economy, more people enter the work force and the supply curve for labor will shift to the right.

Elasticity of the supply and demand curves in labor markets has been the subject of a tremendous amount of research. How sensitive are workers to changes in the wage rate? On one hand, as wage goes up, more workers will make themselves available and those already working will be willing to work more. Students will drop out of or forego college, stay-at-home moms will become second-income earners, and the retired or soon-to-be-retired will work well past their 65th birthdays. This implies the supply curve may be very elastic. On the other hand, most people are happy working 8 hours

---

[11] Marginal product of labor (MP_L) is usually measured in units of output. Marginal revenue product (MRP) is equal to MP_L times price, which is the dollar value of a worker. Some texts will call this "value of marginal product" (VMP) instead of MRP.

Figure 1.10

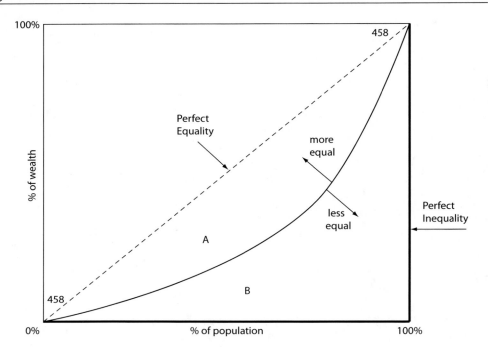

a day, 5 days a week. Small changes in the wage probably will not change people's willingness to work a full-time job. You don't see too many 37-hour weeks. This is due to many factors, including the existence of things like health benefits that are provided by the employer. All of these factors imply the labor supply curve may be relatively inelastic. Both arguments have merit. Estimation of elasticity in labor markets also depends on the industry, the location, and several other factors. Fortunately, for what we will do here, the answer to this debate is largely irrelevant. We will usually assume that changes in wage affect people's willingness to work (i.e., the supply curve is upward sloping). In special cases where it simplifies our lives, we will assume perfectly inelastic supply. Like I said, both have merit.

Income Equality

When we talk about trade and labor markets, the idea of income equality and wealth distributional differences between countries isn't far behind. Which countries have equally distributed income, and which are more unequal? How do we measure this?

This analysis starts with *Lorenz Curves*. Draw a square, then label the x-axis "percent of the population" and label the y-axis "percent of the wealth." Clearly these axes range from zero to 100%, as pictured in Figure 1.10.

Now we order every single person in a country (or location) according to how much they make, from the poorest to the richest. Thus, the first 1% of the population is the poorest 1%, since we have ordered the people this way. We ask each percentile: "What percent of your country's wealth do you earn?" The first group we ask is the poorest 1%, so they can at best make 1% of the wealth. If they make more than 1% of the wealth, then some other group must make less than 1%—which would mean that we didn't order everybody from poorest to richest. So, the first 1% of the population can own between 0% and 1% of the wealth. Then we move on to the second group of 1% of the population, and ask them the same question. With each increment that we move to the right, we are adding one more percent to the population and moving to increasingly wealthy groups. When we arrive at the final group, the top 1% of the population in wealth, we ask how much of the nation's income is theirs. This group can answer anything between 1% (they can't say 0%!) and 100%. If we plot these answers on our graph, we will get some kind of curve as shown above. This curve is called the Lorenz Curve.

Notice that perfect equality has each 1% of the population owning exactly 1% of the wealth, so each movement to the right is accompanied by an equal move upward—mapping out the 45-degree line. In the case of perfect income equality, the Lorenz Curve is the 45-degree line. In the case of perfect inequality, the first 99 groups report that they own 0% of the wealth, so we move to the right and not up at all—until we get to the final group, then we jump up to 100% of the wealth. Thus, the Lorenz Curve for perfect inequality is a right angle that sits atop the outer edge of the box. As a country's income equality becomes more equal, their Lorenz Curve will move toward the 45-degree line. As they become more unequal, the Lorenz Curve is pulled toward the lower right corner of the box.

Although Lorenz Curves give an intuitive method of illustrating income equality between countries, it lacks the precision of numbers. If the United States is more equal than Mexico, then the United States' Lorenz Curve will be above Mexico's. It would be nice if we had a numerical system by which to make this same comparison. Enter the Gini Coefficient.[12] Calculation of the Gini coefficient relies intimately on the Lorenz Curve. The areas in Figure 1.10 are labeled "A" and "B." The formula for the Gini Coefficient is this:

$$Gini = \frac{A}{A+B}$$

The area A+B never changes and is always equal to one half the area of the whole box. Thus the denominator of the fraction above never changes. As a result, this fraction is bound between 0 and 1. As a country's income distribution becomes more equal, the Lorenz Curve will approach the 45-degree line. As this happens, the area labeled "A" will shrink—and so must the Gini Coefficient. Likewise, as a country's

---

[12] Named for Corrado Gini, an Italian statistician.

income distribution becomes more unequal, the Lorenz Curve moves toward the lower right corner, and area "A" grows—and so will the Gini Coefficient. A Gini Coefficient of 0 is perfect equality, and a Gini Coefficient of 1 is perfect inequality. Some Gini Coefficients are listed below.[13] The high and low countries are in bold.

Country	Gini Coefficient
Argentina	0.513
Brazil	0.57
Canada	0.326
China (PRC)	0.469
Denmark	**0.247**
Egypt	0.344
Finland	0.269
France	0.327
Iran	0.43
Ireland	0.343
Italy	0.36
Jamaica	0.455
Japan	0.249
Lithuania	0.36
Mexico	0.461
Norway	0.258
South Africa	**0.578**
South Korea	0.316
Sweden	0.25
United Kingdom	0.36
United States	0.408

---

[13] The Gini Coefficient in the table is measured using data from the United Nations.

Chapter 2

United States Immigration Overview

History of Immigration in the United States

Fortunately for us, the United States has a relatively short history. This makes development of a timeline manageable, although the number of times immigration policy has been changed may still be large enough to surprise you.[1] What follows is a brief timeline of immigration history in the United States.[2] Take note that many (most actually) of these policies are quite exclusive, racist and sort of unbelievable by today's standards. This timeline is not exhaustive or complete. It's just designed to give you an idea about what's gone on over the past 200 years.

1790   Congress adopts uniform rules so that any free white person could apply for citizenship after two years of residency.

1798   Alien and Sedition Acts required 14 years of residency before citizenship and provided for the deportation of "dangerous" aliens.

1800   The term of residency is changed to five years.

1864   Contract Labor Law allowed recruiting of foreign labor.

1868   African Americans gained citizenship with 13th Amendment.

1875   *Henderson v. Mayor of New York* decision declared all state laws governing immigration unconstitutional, stating that Congress must regulate "foreign commerce," of which immigration is a part. Congress also prohibits convicts and prostitutes from entering the country. This is the first federal law limiting immigration qualitatively.

1882   Chinese Exclusion Act—Federal immigration law suspended Chinese immigration for 10 years and barred Chinese already in the United States from citizenship. This Act also barred convicts, lunatics, and others unable to care for themselves from entering the United State. A head tax is also placed on immigrants.

---

[1] Keep in mind, the U.S. has only two geographic neighbors, so the fact that immigration history is so robust implies that something other than location drives migration decisions to migrate.

[2] <http://www.flowofhistory.org>.

1885 Contract Labor Law made it unlawful to import unskilled aliens from overseas as laborers. However, these regulations did not pertain to those crossing land borders.

1888 For the first time since 1798, provisions are adopted for expulsion of aliens.

1890 Foreign-born in United States were 15% of population.

1891 Bureau of Immigration established under the Treasury Department. More classes of aliens restricted including those who were monetarily assisted by others for their passage. Steamship companies were ordered to return ineligible immigrants to countries of origin.

1892 Ellis Island opened to screen immigrants entering on East Coast. (Angel Island screened those on the West Coast, starting in 1910.) Ellis Island officials reported that women traveling alone must be met by a man, or they were immediately deported.

1902 Chinese Exclusion Act renewed indefinitely.

1903 Anarchists, epileptics, polygamists, and beggars ruled inadmissible.

1906 Procedural safeguards enacted for naturalization. Knowledge of English becomes a basic requirement.

1907 Head tax is raised. People with physical or mental defects, tuberculosis, and children unaccompanied by a parent are added to the exclusion list. Japan agreed to limit emigrants to United States in return for elimination of segregating Japanese students in San Francisco schools.

1917 Immigration Act provided for literacy tests for those over 16 and established an "Asiatic Barred Zone," which barred all immigrants from Asia.

1921 Quota Act limited new immigrants to 3% of existing populations for each nationality present in the United States in 1910. This cut Southern and Eastern European immigrants to less than 25% of those in United States before WWI. Asians still barred; no limits on Western hemisphere. Non-quota category established: wives, children of citizens, educated professionals, and domestic servants are no longer counted in quotas.

1922 Japanese made ineligible for citizenship.

1924 Quotas changed to 2% of existing population for each nationality based on numbers in United States in 1890. Based on surnames (many anglicized at Ellis Island) and not the census figures, 82% of all immigrants allowed in the country came from Western and Northern Europe, 16% from Southern and Eastern Europe, 2% from the rest of the world. No distinctions were made between refugees and immigrants, which limited Jewish émigrés during 1930s and 40s. Despite protests from many native people, Native Americans made citizens of the United States. Border Patrol established.

1929 The annual quotas of the 1924 Act are made permanent.

1940 Provided for fingerprinting and registering of all aliens.

1943 In the name of unity among the Allies of WWII, the Chinese Exclusion Laws were repealed, and China's quota was set at a token 105 immigrants annually.

1946 Procedures adopted to facilitate immigration of foreign-born wives, fiancés, husbands, and children of United States armed forces personnel.

1948 Displaced Persons Act allowed 205,000 refugees over two years; gave priority to Baltic States refugees; admitted as quota immigrants.

1950 The grounds for exclusion and deportation are expanded. All aliens required to report their addresses annually.

1952 Immigration and Nationality Act eliminated race as a bar to immigration or citizenship. Japan's quota was set at 185 annually. China's stayed at 105; other Asian countries were given 100 each. Northern and Western Europe's quota was placed at 85% of all immigrants. Tighter restrictions were placed on immigrants coming from British colonies in order to stem the tide of black West Indians entering under Britain's generous quota. Non-quota class enlarged to include husbands of American women.

1953 The 1948 refugee law expanded to admit 200,000 above the existing limit.

1965 Hart-Celler Act abolished national origins quotas, establishing separate ceilings for the Eastern (170,000) and Western (120,000) hemispheres (revised in 1976 and combined in 1978). Categories of preference based on family ties, critical skills, diversity, and refugee status.

1978 Separate ceilings for Western and Eastern hemispheric immigration combined into a worldwide limit of 290,000.

1980 The Refugee Act removes refugees as a preference category; reduces worldwide ceiling for immigration to 270,000.

1986 Immigration Reform and Control Act addresses the issues of unauthorized immigration by sanctioning employers who knowingly hire or recruit unauthorized aliens. Provided amnesty for many illegal aliens. Amnesty details allow for agricultural workers present since 1982 (about 2.7 million) to become legal residents.

1989 A bill gives permanent status to registered nurses who have lived in United States for at least three years and met established certification standards.

1990 Immigration Act limited unskilled workers to 10,000/year; skilled labor requirements and immediate family reunification major goals. Policy continued to promote nuclear family model, with the addition of categorical admission to promote diversity. Worldwide cap increased to 675,000. Foreign-born in United States was 7%.

1996 The Illegal Immigration Reform and Responsibility Act designed primarily to limit welfare consumption by immigrants.

2001   United States Patriot Act amended the Immigration and Nationality Act to broaden the scope of aliens ineligible for admission or deportable due to terrorist activities to include an alien who: (1) is a representative of a political, social, or similar group whose political endorsement of terrorist acts undermines United States antiterrorist efforts; (2) has used a position of prominence to endorse terrorist activity, or to persuade others to support such activity in a way that undermines United States antiterrorist efforts (or the child or spouse of such an alien under specified circumstances); or (3) has been associated with a terrorist organization and intends to engage in threatening activities while in the United States.

2010   Arizona bill SB1070 makes it a violation of state law to be in the state of Arizona without legal status.

Of particular importance from the above list are the qualitative restrictions of 1875, the introduction and revision of the quota system 1921 (and 1924), and the policies of 1965 (updates in 1976 and 1978) eliminating country-of-origin quotas in favor of a family-based system. For almost a century, the qualitative characteristics of immigrants were used as the basis for admission to the United States after the passage of the 1875 law. Although these restrictions evolved over time, things like job skills, education, and criminal record (or lack thereof) were the factors that rationed admission. Numerical restrictions in the 1920s strengthened the restrictions of United States policy. These restrictions remained the standard until 1965, at which point the focus of immigration policy became family reunification. In addition, the abolition of quotas made possible greater immigration from certain areas. It is important to note that quotas based on country of origin were abolished, but a total cap of the number of immigrants admitted remained (and does to this day). These 1965 changes have contributed profoundly to the demographics of the United States' population and they continue to affect ongoing immigration issues.

Some of the policies listed above must sound ridiculous to you today. For example, the Chinese Exclusion Act (1882 and 1902), which prohibited immigration from China and forbade those already in the United States from citizenship, or similar measures against Japanese immigrants in 1922, would be unheard of in today's open political climate. Likewise, the fact that women traveling alone had to be met by a man to avoid deportation (1892) is absurd by today's standards. However, it is important to recognize how perverse immigration policy has been historically in order to make intelligent contributions to ongoing policy debate. In addition, it is clear that many of the policies we have used in the past are not designed with economic performance in mind—it certainly can't be optimal to eliminate all immigrants from a single country without concern for their economic potential. For example, the removal of the Chinese ban was due to political wartime alliances (China and the United States were allies in WWII), not for economic reasons.

Overview of Terms

Here are some terms we will use with regularity. *Alien* refers to anybody who is not a citizen but has arrived here and somehow gained admission. I say "somehow" because admission obviously does not have to be legal, as we will see. Lawful admission to the United States is separated into two different categories: permanent and temporary. Technically, only legal permanent admission warrants use of the term *immigrant*, but for most purposes, *immigrant* is synonymous with the term *foreign-born*. For example, the term "illegal immigrant" should really be "illegal alien," but we won't split hairs in this text.[3] The reason for the high degree of technical difficulty of terms is due to the fact that much of this terminology is pulled from legal or quasi-legal documents produced by government agencies.

Aliens granted permanent legal status are called Legal (or Lawful) Permanent Residents (LPRs). Having LPR status is equivalent to having a "green card." This allows you to live, work, and travel freely in the United States, but certain privileges (such as voting) are still withheld until citizenship is obtained. Yes, the cards were in fact green historically, giving rise to the name. (In 2010, a green version was issued again.) LPRs then must satisfy additional requirements concerning time spent in the United States, et cetera, prior to being granted citizenship. Citizenship is no longer withheld from anybody—if you're patient enough to go through the process, then you can become a United States citizen regardless of where you're from or what you do for a living. However, an immigrant can never become a native. This is an obvious fact that you may actually have to keep in mind later.

Some Statistics

Since the Homeland Security Act of 2002, immigration matters are handled by the Department of Homeland Security, which is further broken down into the United States Citizenship and Immigration Service, the Bureau of Customs and Border Protection, the Bureau of Immigration and Customs Enforcement, and the United States Coast Guard. Each Bureau is responsible for slightly different aspects (with some overlap) of immigration enforcement. Despite this, data tend to coalesce centrally at the Department of Homeland Security. Prior to 2001, the Immigration and Naturalization Service (INS) was responsible for immigration matters and data

---

[3] We will also use the terms "unauthorized," "unlawful," et cetera.

Figure 2.1

collection. In addition, the Bureau of the Census provides a valuable source of data, but with lags of ten years.

Using census data, we begin with a quick look at how the United States immigrant population has evolved over the past 100 years. As you interpret Figure 2.2, try to bear in mind any significant events that coincide with peaks and valleys of the graph (like wars, the Great Depression, changes in immigration policy, NAFTA, et cetera).

Recall that "foreign-born" is technically different from "immigrant" in that a foreign-born person does not have to possess LPR status. Some of fluctuation in the diagram above may in fact be driven by illegal immigration or by temporary visitors to the United States for example. (Whether or not these people show up on census survey data is a topic to be discussed later.) Already your mind may be spinning about the fact that some groups of people (e.g., illegal immigrants) may not fully be represented by census data due to the illegal nature of their arrival or stay. You're right, and this is a problem that we will revisit often.

Compare Figure 2.2 to Figure 2.3, which shows the number of LPRs in the United States over the past two centuries. It appears that the major peaks (1900 to 1920) and valleys (around 1950) reflect those in Figure 2.2, although the match isn't perfect. For example, the biggest valley in Figure 2.2 occurs somewhere near 1970, while the corresponding dip in Figure 2.3 seems to occur around 1940—probably due to WWII. What might explain this apparent inconsistency? I would conjecture that new LPRs stopped coming in the 1940s, but the existing foreign-born didn't die off right away—they continued to live and age here in the United States until the 1970s. As you can see, details about terminology (e.g., LPR vs. foreign-born) may be important enough to affect how we interpret data on immigration, so be careful.

The peak represented by a dashed line at 1986 is thanks to a policy that essentially gave amnesty to illegal immigrants who had been working in the United States for a

---

[4] Hanson, "Why Does Immigration Divide America?" p. 13.

Figure 2.2

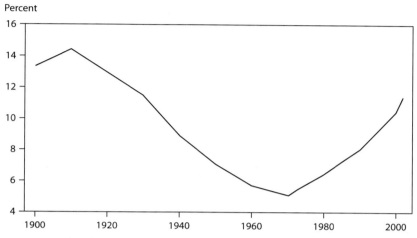

Share of the foreign-born in the US population, 1900–2003

Percent

Source: US Census of Population and Housing, various years.

Figure 2.3[4]

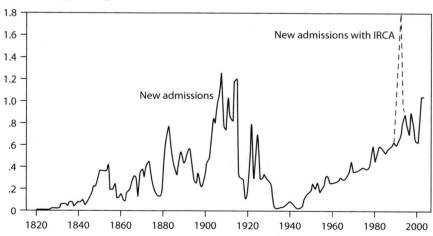

Permanent Legal Immigration to the United States, 1820–2000 (millions of people)

Permanent Legal Immigration

New admissions with IRCA

New admissions

IRCA = Immigration Reform and Control Act (1986)

Source: U.S. Department of Homeland Security, Office of Immigration Statistics, *2003 Yearbook of Immigration Statistics*.

Table 2.1

Permanent (Immigrant) Admissions, by Category of New Arrival, 1996 to 2004									
	1996	1997	1998	1999	2000	2001	2002	2003	2004
Number of New Admission, by Type									
First-time entry to the United States	431,405	380,719	357,037	401,755	407,402	411,059	384,427	358,411	362.221
Adjustment of status to LPR	494,495	417,659	297,414	244,793	442,405	653,259	679,305	347,416	583,921
Total	915,900	798,378	654,451	646,568	849,807	1,064,318	1,063,732	705,827	946,412
Percentage of New Admissions, by Type									
First-time entry to the United States	46	48	55	62	48	39	36	51	38
Adjustment of status to LPR	54	52	45	38	52	61	64	49	62

Source: Congressional Budget Office based on Department of Homeland Security, Office of Immigration Statistics, 2004 Yearbook of Immigration Statistics (January 2006).

certain period of time. Nearly 2.7 million illegal immigrant workers present since 1982 were allowed to become legal permanent residents. However, these workers were not new entrants, which is why the diagram differentiates this group from the other LPRs.

Recently, the number of lawful immigrants has hovered in the ballpark of one million new LPRs per year and is in the area of five million for temporary visas. However, these numbers can be misleading. The fact that there are one million LPRs in a given year does not actually mean that one million people legally crossed the border that year. Many of these LPRs may in fact be adjustments from temporary to permanent status. As Table 2.1 implies, some years the majority of newly issued LPRs are adjustments.

In addition to LPRs and temporary visa holders, there is also a large group of visitors admitted as part of a visa waiver program (for example, Canadians visiting the United States). In these cases, a person's passport serves in lieu of an issued visa. These numbers are in the area of 15 to 16 million per year.

We also need to account for those immigrants who are here illegally. One important thing to realize is that not all illegal immigrants cross the border in the middle of the night through the desert. In fact, a large percentage (about half) of the unauthorized immigrant population consists of people who originally arrived legally but have overstayed the terms of a temporary visa. In either case, counting illegal immigrants is actually quite difficult to do given the nature of their entry or stay. Estimates of how many unauthorized or illegal immigrants are currently in the United States range from 7 million to over 12 million.[5] This number represents only a fraction of the total immigrant population (albeit a large fraction), but is definitely too large to ignore. We will revisit illegal immigration later in the text.

---

[5] E.g. U.S. Census Bureau and the INS.

Interestingly, data on exits by immigrants are not well kept.[6] (The Bureau of the Census estimates an average of 217,000 LPR exits annually.) In addition, many illegal immigrants do not stay in the United States permanently. For example, many immigrant workers from Mexico return home for a portion of the year (typically winter, when agricultural employment declines in the United States). These issues are all major obstacles to estimating the number of foreign-born living in the United States.

If we could account for every foreign-born individual somehow, we would find the following:

Total number of foreign born =

$\sum$*New LPRs + Adjustments to LPR status + Illegal immigrants*
+ Temporary visas + Visa waivers - Deaths - Exits

The sum is taken over time, probably a period long enough to capture the life expectancy of a person. A version of this method has been used to estimate the number of illegal immigrants in the United States (see Passel, 2005). Unfortunately, we keep data on only three or four of these categories: New LPRs, Adjustments to LPR status, Temporary visas, and possibly Deaths. Notice that the categories for which we keep data are among the smallest groups on the list. This data issue will resurface periodically as a challenge to empirical work in the field of immigration.

Overview of Current Immigration Policy in the United States

Current policy in the United States is essentially a remnant of the policies established in 1965 and then amended in 1976 and 1978. Gone are the quota systems from the first half of the 20th century. In fact, current policy tends in the opposite direction: since the Immigration Act of 1990, there are categorical admissions designed to promote diversity. There is, however, a cap of 675,000 total immigrants admitted, regardless of country of origin, with unused spots rolling over to the following year.

The goals of the current United States policy are relatively vague, as the summary below shows:

1. To reunite families by admitting immigrants who already have family members living in the United States;
2. To admit workers in occupations with strong demand for labor;
3. To provide a refuge for people who face the risk of political, racial, or religious persecution in their home countries; and
4. To provide admission to people from a diverse set of countries.

Summary data for the early part of this decade are presented in Table 2.2.[7]

---

[6] If an immigrant emigrates, are they still an immigrant?

[7] "Immigration Policy in the United States," Congressional Budget Office, February 2006.

Table 2.2

Lawful Admissions and Issuances of Visas, 2000 to 2004

(Thousands)

	2000	2001	2002	2003	2004
Admissions of Lawful Permanent Residents	**Permanent (Immigrant) Admissions**				
Unrestricted					
Immediate Relatives of U.S. Citizens	348	443	486	333	406
Generally restricted					
Family-sponsored preference admissions	235	232	187	159	214
Employment-sponsored preference admissions	107	179	175	82	155
Refugees and asylum-seekers	66	109	126	45	71
Diversity admissions	51	42	43	46	50
Other	43	59	47	41	49
Total	**850**	**1,064**	**1,064**	**706**	**946**
	Temporary (Nonimmigrant) Admissions and Issuances				
Visa Issuances	7,142	7,589	5,769	4,882	5,049
Admissions Under the Visa Waiver Program (Includes multiple entries)	17,595	16,471	13,113	13,490	15,762

Source: Congressional Budget Office based on Department of Justice, Immigratioin and Naturalization Service, *2001 Statistical Yearbook of the Immigration and Naturalization Service* (Februrary 2003); Department of Homeland Security, Office of Immigratioin Statistics, *2003 Yearbook of Immigration Statistics* (September 2004) and *2004 Yearbook of Immigration Statistics* (January 2006); and Department of State, Bureau of Consular Affairs, *Report of the Visa Office 2003*, available at http://travel.state.gov/visa/about/report/report_2750.html.

Family-based Immigration

In keeping with the goal of family reunification, spouses of citizens, parents of adult citizens (at least 21 years old), and unmarried children (under 21) of citizens are admitted without limit. In 2004, 43% of LPRs were in this category. In addition to immediate family, a United States citizen can sponsor more-distant family members who are admitted with limits according the preference ordering summarized in Table 2.3. Notice that immigration policy promotes a nuclear family in allowing spouses, parents, and children to precede more-distant relatives.

Work-based Immigration

There are currently five employment-based categories from which a person may be admitted into the United States:

1. Priority workers with extraordinary ability in the arts, athletics, business, education, or science;
2. Professionals holding advanced degrees;
3. Workers in occupations deemed to be experiencing shortages;
4. Religious and other special workers;
5. People willing to invest at least $1 million in business within the United States.

Table 2.3[8]

Numerical Ceilings and Admissions, by Immigration Category, 2004

Category	Total ceiling		Admissions
	Ceilling	Special Additions	
Immediate Relatives of U.S. Citizens	Not subject to ceiling		406,074
Family-Based Immigration			
First preference: Unmarried adult (Ages 21 and older) sons and daughters of U.S. citizens	23,400	Plus visas not required for fourth preference	26,380
Second prefernece: Spouses and dependent children and unmarried sons and daughters of LPRs	114,200	Plus visas not required for first preference	93,609
Third preference: Married sons and daughters of U.S. citizens	23,400	Plus visas not required for first or second preference	28,695
Fourth preference: Siblings ages 21 and older of U.S. citizens	65,000	Plus visas not required for first, second, or third preference	65,671
Subtotal	**226,000**		**214,355**
Employment-Based Immigration			
First preference: Priority workers	58,465	Plus unused visas from fourth and fifth preference categories	31,291
Second preference: Members of the professions	58,465	Plus unused first preference visas	32,534
Third preference: Skilled and unskilled shortage workers	58,464	Plus unused visas from the first or second preference categories; 10,000 of these are reserved for unskilled workers	58,969
Fourth preference: Special immigrants	14,514		5,407
Fifth preference: Employment-creation investors	14,514		129
Sub total	**204,422**		**155,330**
Diversity Program Participants	50,000		50,084
Asylum-Seekers		No limit on receiving; limit of 10,000 on LPR adjustments	10,016
Refugees	70,000	Presidential determination; no limit on LPR adjustments	61,013
Other		Dependent on specific adjustment authority	49,270
Total Overall Admissions	**N.A.**		**946,142**

Approximately 16% of LPRs were in one of these five categories; over half of these were in group #3. The process for work-based immigration begins with the employer's filing a request with the Department of Labor. Once approved, a second petition must be filed with the Citizenship and Immigration Service. Table 2.3 summarizes total admissions for this group.

Refugees' Immigration

Refugees and asylum-seekers (people unable or unwilling to return to their home countries for fear of racial, religious or political persecution) comprised 8% of total LPRs in 2004. The number of refugees admitted to the United States is determined by

---

[8] "Immigration Policy in the United States," Congressional Budget Office, February 2006.

the President (with input from Congress), and is typically set to cover at least half of the world population identified as refugees by the United Nations.

Other Immigration

Temporary, non-immigrant visas total approximately five million and include groups like tourists, business people, and visitors. These are summarized in Table 2.4. The largest category of visas issued were H visas, issued for employment (H visas require labor certification). Of these, the most common subcategory is H1-B, used for temporary workers in professional specialties. In addition, nearly 16 million people were admitted via the visa waiver program. In this program, citizens of 27 participating countries may enter the United States without a visa for visits of 90 days or less.[9] The person's passport serves as the substitute for a visa in this situation. See Table 2.4 for a summary of these and other visa admissions.

Diversity-based Immigration

The remaining group of LPRs was admitted as part of the diversity program introduced in 1990. Up to 50,000 people from historically underrepresented countries, primarily in Africa (41%) and Europe (38%), are admitted via a State Department lottery. The article on page 40, taken from the *Wall Street Journal*, comments on the recent uptick in popularity of the State Department lottery.

From LPR to Citizen

Attaining LPR status is not the end of the road for immigrants. If additional conditions are satisfied, as summarized in Table 2.5[10], LPRs can eventually become citizens. Why would an immigrant consider additional steps needed for citizenship? For one, citizenship carries with it additional privileges like voting. Also, citizenship cannot be revoked, does not expire, and is maintenance-free—all qualities that are unique to citizenship. In Figure 2.4 is an image of a 2010 green card. Note the existence of an expiration date.[11]

---

[9] Andorra, Australia, Austria, Belgium, Brunei, Denmark, Finland, France, Germany, Iceland, Ireland, Italy, Japan, Liechtenstein, Luxembourg, Monaco, the Netherlands, New Zealand, Norway, Portugal, San Marino, Singapore, Slovenia, Spain, Sweden, Switzerland, and the United Kingdom.

[10] "Immigration Policy in the United States," Congressional Budget Office, February 2006.

[11] Image taken from <http://www.green-card.com/Green-Card-Lottery/how-to-get-a-greencard.html> on 1/24/11. Although not clear when printed in black and white, the card is actually green.

Figure 2.4

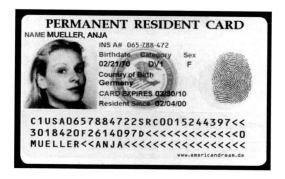

Table 2.4[12]

Number and Type of Nonimmigrant (Temporary) Visa Issuances, 1992 to 2003

Type of Temporary Admission	visa Class	2000	2001	2002	2003
Temporary Visitor (Excluding Visa Waiver Program)					
Business	B-1	75,919	84,201	75,642	60,892
Pleasure	B-2	509,031	381,431	255,487	271,358
Business and Pleasure	B-1/B-2	3,567,580	3,527,118	2,528,103	2,207,303
Combination B-1/B-2 and border-crossing card	B-1/B-2/BCC	1,510,133	1,990,402	1,399,819	836,407
Subtotal		**5,662,663**	**5,983,152**	**4,259,051**	**3,375,960**
Official Representative and Immediate Family	A.G	117,609	111,165	117,115	114,606
Transitional Family Member	K	24,746	28,712	39,008	44,633
Student	F-1, M-1	290,160	298,730	238,438	219,852
Spouse or child of Student	F-2, M-2	25,339	26,445	22,373	20,029
Subtotal		**315,499**	**325,175**	**260,811**	**239,881**
Intracompany Trensferee	L-1	54,963	59,384	57,721	57,245
Spouse or Child of Intracompany Transferee	L-2	57,069	61,154	54,903	53,571
Exchange Visitor	J-1	236,837	261,769	253,841	253,866
Spouse or Child of Exchange Visitor	J-2	37,122	38,189	32,539	29,796
Subtotal		**273,959**	**299,958**	**286,380**	**283,662**
NAFTA Professional	TN	906	787	699	423
Spouse or Child of NAFTA Professional	TD	1,128	1,041	856	796
Temporary Worker					
Registered nurse	H-1A	2			
Worker of distinguished merit and ability	H-1B	133,290	161,643	118,352	107,196
Nurse in shortage area	H-1X		34	212	191
Worker in agricultural services	H-2A	30,201	31,523	31,538	29,882
Worker in other services	H-2B	45,037	58,215	62,591	78,955
Trainee	H-3	1,514	1,613	1,387	1,417
Spouse or child of temporary worker	H-4	79,518	95,967	79,725	69,289
Subtotal		**289,562**	**348,995**	**293,805**	**286,930**
Worker with Extraordinary Ability in Sciences, Arts, etc.	0-1, 0-2	8,360	8,584	7,998	8,598
Internationally Recognized Athlete or Entertainer	P-1, P-2, P-3	34,525	32,998	32,537	33,463
Spouse or Child of Certain Foreign Worker	0-3, P-4	2,969	3,307	2,698	2,447
Cultural Exchange or Religious Worker	Q-1, Q-2, R-1	9,800	10,121	10,444	10,604
Spouse or Child of Cultural Exchange or Religious Worker	Q-3, R-2	2,492	3,195	3,176	3,164
Treaty Trader or Treaty Investor and Spouse and Children	E	36,520	36,886	33,444	32,096
International Media and Spouse and Children	I	13,928	13,799	18,187	12,329
Total		**7,141,636**	**7,588,778**	**5,769,437**	**4,881,632**

Source: Congressional Budget Office based on Department of Homeland Security, Office of Immigration Statistics, 2003 yearbook of *Immigration Statistics* (Spetember 2004); Alison Siskin, *Visa Waiver Program*, CRS Report for Congress RL32221 (Congressional Research Service, April 19, 2005); and Department of State, Bureau of Consular Affirs, *Report of the Visa Office, 1996* (April 1997), *Report of the Visa Office, 2000*, available at http://travel.state.gov/pdf/FY2000_TOC.pdf, and *Report of the Visa Office, 2003*, http://travel.state.gov/visa/about/report/report_2750.html.

---

[12] "Immigration Policy in the United States," Congressional Budget Office, February 2006.

Table 2.5

Requirements for Naturalization

| Characteristics of Applicant | Preconditions | | | |
	Time as Lawful Permanent Resident	Continuous Residence in the United States	Physical Presence in the United States	Time in District/State
Lawful Permanent Residents with No Special Circumstances	Five years	Five years	30 months	Three months
Married to and Living with a U.S. Citizen for the Past Three Years; Spouse Must Have Been a Citizen for the Past Three Years	Three years	Three years	18 months	Three months
In the Armed Forces for at Least One Year	Must be an LPR at the time of interview	Not required	Not required	Not required
In the Armed Forces for Less than One Year, or in the Armed Forces Less than One Year and Discharged More than Six Months Earlier	Five years	Five years	30 months	Three months
Performed Active Military Duty During World War I, World War II, Korea, Vietnam, Persian Gulf, on or After September 11, 2001	Not required	Not required	Not required	Not required
Widow or Widower of a U.S. Citizen Who Died During Active Duty	Must be an LPR at the time of interview	Not required	Not required	Not required
Employee of, or Under Contract to, U.S. Government	Five years	Five years	30 months	Three months
Performing Ministerial or Priestly Functions for a Religious Denomination or an Interdenominational Organization with a Valid U.S. Presence	Five years	Five years	30 months	Three months
Employed by Certain U.S. Research Institutions, a U.S.-Owned Firm Involved with Development of U.S. Foreign Trade or Commerce, or Public International Organizations of Which the United States Is a Member	Five years	Five years	30 months	Three months
Employed for Five Years or More by a U.S. Nonprofit Organization Supporting U.S. Interests Abroad Through Communications Media	Five years	Not required	Not required	Not required
Spouse of a U.S. Citizen Who Is a Member of the Armed Forces, or in One of the Four Previous Categories, and Who Is Working Abroad Under an Employment Contract with a Qualifying Employer for at Least One Year (Including the Time at Which the Applicant Naturalizes)	Must be an LPR at the time of interview	Not required	Not required	Not required

Source: Congressional Budget Office based on Department of Homeland Security, U.S. Citizenship and Immigration Services, *A Guide to Naturalization* (February 2004).

Green-Card Lottery Record

*15 Million Seek to Settle in U.S. Through
Visa Program That Leaves It to Chance*

By Miriam Jordan
Wall Street Journal, November 22, 2010

A record 15 million people around the world this year entered America's green-card lottery, an immigration program that offers a quick path to legal, permanent U.S. residence for 50,000 people a year—selected purely by the luck of the draw.

The so-called "diversity visa program" lottery drew nearly 25% more entries than last year, according to the State Department. The limit of 50,000 green-card recipients through the program was established years ago by Congress. Some lawmakers are now calling for an end to the program.

The annual lottery creates a buzz across the developing world. Applicants from Kenya to Khazakstan brave lines at Internet kiosks to fill out electronic entries. In the final hours of the month-long enrollment period, which this year closed Nov. 3, entries were rolling in at the rate of 62,000 an hour.

Recent winners already in the U.S. include cab drivers, professional athletes, Internet entrepreneurs and military personnel.

Luck of the Draw

More people are entering the green-card lottery . . .

Total entrants into the lottery*

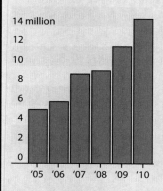

. . . with the largest number from Bangladesh . . .

Top five countries in the most recent lottery

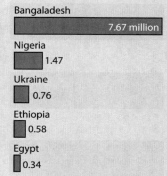

. . . though the share of immigrants through the lottery remains small.

Legal permanent resident flow by category of admission, 2009

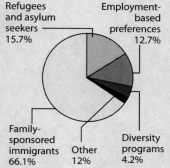

*Winners who enter the lottery is fall 2010 will receive their visas to focal year 2012

Sources: State Dept. of Homeland security

"I would never have started a company that created value in the United States if I haven't won the lottery," said Adam Gries, a 29-year-old Israeli who runs an Internet start up in San Francisco. "I would be creating companies in Israel."

Critics say the program poses security risks, lures uneducated immigrants and enables individuals with no connection to the U.S. to get into the country more quickly than those sponsored by relatives and employers.

"More and more people are learning about this program and are dumbfounded that we have it in the first place," said Rep. Bob Goodlatte (R., Va.), who has introduced legislation to abolish it. "Our chances have never been better to kill it," he added, following his party's successes in the midterm elections and amid high unemployment in the U.S.

Launched in 1990 to promote diversity in the immigrant population, the green-card lottery is now open to people from almost anywhere in the world, except countries that already boast a large number of nationals in the U.S., including Mexico, China, India and the Philippines. No special skills are required: A high-school diploma suffices. Lottery winners eventually qualify for U.S. citizenship.

The number of entries has been rising each year. This year's total is more than 2.5 times greater than five years ago, when the lottery attracted 5.5 million entries. Immigration scholars say possible reasons include the spread of Internet connectivity and increased awareness of the lottery, which costs nothing to enter.

"There is no faster way to get a green card to come to the United States," said Mark Jacobsen, an immigration lawyer. "The American dream is held out as a torch in the entire world."

In Africa and Asia, banners advertising the lottery festoon remote villages and teeming city alleys, where Internet cafes do brisk business helping applicants fill out entry forms, which must be completed online.

In flood-prone Bangladesh, "it seems everyone in the country knows about it," said Sandra Ingram, consular chief in Dhaka, who holds news conferences during lottery season.

After an electronic draw, about 100,000 applicants will be notified in May—twice as many as ultimately will be eligible to move in the U.S.—to undergo interviews, background checks and medical exams.

There is no cap on how many times the same person can enter the lottery—but no country can represent more than 7% of the total visas issued in a given year. For the fiscal year ended Sept. 30, 2009, nationals from Ethiopia, Egypt and Nigeria were the top recipients. This year, Bangladesh and Nigeria supplied the most entries.

Five years since arriving as a single man in San Diego, lottery winner Tsegaye Kedir of Ethiopia is married and a U.S. citizen preparing to attend college.

"I came because the U.S. has big opportunity for work, to get an education and to live a better life than in my country," said the 29-year-old, who drives a taxi.

Zoltan Mesko, a rookie punter with the New England Patriots, came to the U.S. from Romania thanks to the program, after his family won a spot in the lottery when he was a child. Hundreds of winners have gone on to enlist in the U.S. armed forces.

Although the program accounts for a small percentage of the million or so legal immigrants who enter the U.S. each year, critics say it diverts scarce State Department resources from processing more important visa categories.

"It shows that the U.S. immigration system doesn't make sense," said Bernard Wolfsdorf, an immigration attorney. "We are allocating visas based on luck instead of knowledge."

Rep. Goodlatte of Virginia and others also voice concern that the program is inviting to terrorists, because people don't need to prove they have ties to the U.S. and are guaranteed permanent residency, which allows them to get almost any job—even handling explosives.

Hesham Mohammed Ali Hedayet, an Egyptian who killed two people at an El Al airline counter in Los Angles in 2002, was able to remain in the U.S. after overstaying his visitor's visa because his wife won the green-card lottery.

The State Department said those who get in through the lottery are subjected to the same stringent security review as other vise applicants.

Margaret Stock, a retired West Point professor who studies immigration and defense, said terrorists wouldn't be stopped by abolishing the program. "The DV lottery is not any more susceptible to terrorism than other visa programs," Lt. Col. Stock said.

Egyptian-born Mohammed Atta, one of the hijackers in the Sept. 11, 2001 terrorist attacks, entered the green-card lottery at least once, according to documents reviewed by *The Wall Street Journal*. He never won a spot in the lottery, and eventually came to the U.S. on a business-visitor visa instead.

Fraud is another challenge. The fervor for a shot at the American Dream prompted one Bangladeshi man to submit 2,800 entries, the State Department said; just one entry per year is allowed.

But if an entrant is disqualified one year, he or she can still enter the next year.

"All is forgiven, it's a new lottery," said one U.S. official.

As the article below shows, however, there may be a difference between how a policy is written and how it is executed.

Soldier Finds Minefield on Road to Citizenship

By Miriam Jordan
Wall Street Journal, February 10, 2011

During 10 years in the U.S. Army, Luis Lopez served in Iraq and Afghanistan, earned medals and had a commander laud his service as a "critical part of the success of his unit fighting the global war on terrorism."

Mr. Lopez is also an illegal immigrant. In late December, the staff sergeant was discharged from the Army after applying for U.S. citizenship. And because of his illegal status, the 28-year-old native of Mexico couldn't work as he waited for immigration authorities to decide if he would be granted citizenship or find himself at risk of deportation.

Mr. Lopez's case reflects the federal government's complex—and seemingly inconsistent—relationship with illegal immigrants in the armed forces. Illegal immigrants aren't allowed to voluntarily enlist for active duty. Yet if they find a way to join, a section of the Immigration and Naturalization Act provides them a path to citizenship.

The 1952 immigration law says foreign nationals who have "served honorably" during wartime may be naturalized "whether or not [they have been] lawfully admitted to the United States for permanent residence."

That statute drew attention in December when Sen. Jeff Sessions (R., Ala.) referred to it ahead of the defeat in Congress of the Dream Act, part of which would give some illegal immigrants a legal status that would enable them to enlist and eventually gain citizenship.

The Dream Act isn't needed, he wrote, because "there is already a legal process in place for illegal aliens to obtain U.S. citizenship through military service."

The 1952 law has allowed some illegal immigrants in the military to become U.S. citizens, though how many isn't clear. And citizenship isn't guaranteed: It can turn on decisions made deep within the military bureaucracy.

Pfc. Juan Escalante of Seattle joined the Army using a fake green card and fought in Iraq. In 2003, Pfc. Escalante confessed that he had used fraudulent documents. The military allowed him to stay, and the U.S. gave him citizenship.

In her four years in the Air Force, Liliana Plata of Los Angeles won medals and promotions. In 2008, she was discharged after the military discovered she used another person's identity to enlist. In December 2010, U.S. Immigration and Citizenship Services denied her application for citizenship. A spokeswoman said the agency cannot comment on individual cases.

Between September 2001 and September 2010, 64,643 members of the armed forces were naturalized by the agency. The agency doesn't track how many came to the U.S. illegally.

The military supports the Dream Act, and military officials say more stringent scrutiny of identification has made it difficult for illegal immigrants to enlist in recent years. "We don't knowingly allow illegal immigrants to enlist," said George Wright, an Army spokesman.

But immigration attorneys say the practice is widespread, in part because of the lure of citizenship.

"Fraud enlistments are pretty common, and the government can deal with this in many ways. If they don't want to discharge, there are a dozen ways to look the other way," said John Quinn, an immigration attorney in San Diego who was previously involved in processing fraud enlistments for the Marines.

Luis Lopez was 8 years old when his parents brought him to the U.S. from Mexico in 1990. They overstayed their tourist visas and fell out of legal status.

Mr. Lopez says he visited an Army recruitment office in suburban Los Angles to enlist after finishing high school. The recruiter said he couldn't join unless until he presented a green card or birth certificate, says Mr. Lopez.

A few weeks later, Mr. Lopez says he gave the recruiter a fake "birth abstract" that stated he was born in Los Angeles County. "That was it," he said. "I went straight to Korea for a year."

He was also deployed to Iraq twice and then to Afghanistan, from early 2009 to 2010. He collected more than a dozen accolades for his service. The paratrooper's latest Army commendation medal was awarded for his service in Afghanistan, where he was section chief for an airborne field artillery battalion's radar system that tracked incoming enemy fire.

Mr. Lopez says after returning to his base in Fort Richardson, Alaska, last summer he informed his supervisors that he was an illegal immigrant and was taking steps to apply for citizenship. He continued to report to work on the base.

In August, he began filling out immigration forms to rectify his status. One form required the personnel department on the base to attest that Mr. Lopez was serving "honorably," to qualify him for citizenship.

Sharon Harris, chief of the division, raised questions over the fact he had presented a counterfeit document to enlist, says Mr. Lopez. In September, Ms. Harris checked the "No" box beside the statement, "Applicant served honorably or is currently serving honorably."

In response to emailed questions, an Army spokesman wrote that Ms. Harris had checked "No" because Sgt. Lopez had "fraudulently enlisted."

The Army initiated procedures to discharge him.

On Dec. 22, Mr. Lopez received his official discharge form, which states he was discharged due to "fraudulent entry." Still, the form described his service as "honorable." Mr. Lopez then submitted a copy of the form to immigration officials.

Mr. Lopez's commanding officer, Lt. Col. Frank Stanco, provided a recommendation letter for the immigration agency stating, "I strongly recommend that SSG Lopez [be] awarded United States Citizenship for his commitment and service to the United States of America."

Mr. Lopez heard nothing about his application for citizenship until about 10 days after the *Wall Street Journal* put questions to immigration authorities. Late Thursday, his lawyer, Neil O'Donnell, received word that Mr. Lopez would be granted citizenship. He took part in a naturalization ceremony Wednesday and is now a citizen.

Mr. Lopez could now try to re-enlist in the Army. After his ordeal, he said: "I'm still thinking about it."

Illegal Immigration

It has been estimated that over half of immigrants from Mexico to the United States lack proper documentation. For groups not coming from Mexico, the number is nearly 20%. Although there is debate about how to best estimate a population that intentionally tries to avoid being counted, most figures are at least in the same ballpark—near 10 million. With these estimates, it is understandable that illegal immigration is a serious topic of immigration debate.

Any person present in the United States without a valid (i.e., not expired) visa or green card is illegal. If caught, violators can be fined, imprisoned, prohibited from

Table 2.6

		Formal Removals			
	Apprehensions	Nonexpedited	Expedited	Total	Voluntary Departures
Enforcement Efforts, 1991 to 2004					
1991	1,197,875	33,189	n.a.	33,189	1,061,105
1992	1,258,481	43,671	n.a.	43,671	1,105,829
1993	1,327,261	42,542	n.a.	42,542	1,243,410
1994	1,094,719	45,674	n.a.	45,674	1,029,107
1995	1,394,554	50,924	n.a.	50,924	1,313,764
1996	1,649,986	69,680	n.a.	69,680	1,573,428
1997	1,536,520	91,190	23,242	114,432	1,440,684
1998	1,679,439	97,068	76,078	173,146	1,570,127
1999	1,714,035	91,902	89,170	181,072	1,574,682
2000	1,814,729	100,296	85,926	186,222	1,675,711
2001	1,387,486	108,185	69,841	178,026	1,254,035
2002	1,062,279	116,006	34,536	150,542	934,119
2003	1,046,422	145,610	43,758	189,368	887,115
2004	1,241,089	161,090	41,752	202,842	1,035,477

re-entry, or merely allowed to leave voluntarily.[13] Just over 200,000 people are formally removed each year, while about one million depart voluntarily. Keep in mind the fact that visitors overstaying the term of their visas are classified as unauthorized aliens—illegal immigration is not limited to people sneaking over a border in the middle of the night. An overview of apprehensions and departures is presented in Table 2.6.

It is clear from the numbers in Table 2.6 and from the estimates of how many illegal immigrants are in the United States that we are not very successful in apprehending illegal immigrants. If we believe that there are 10 to 15 million illegal immigrants here now, then we have an apprehension rate that is around 10%. Those are pretty good odds for immigrants. Why are we so bad at catching people who are not authorized to live or work in the United States? I'm sure you can imagine that the search for illegal immigrants should be relatively straight-forward—as we will see later, immigrants (both legal and illegal) tend to congregate in only a few areas in the United States, typically near the largest cities. (We will later identify six "immigrant states" where over 70% of total immigrant population is located.) Why such a dismal rate of success? It's intentional. In fact, you can view the low apprehension rate as part of the United States' immigration policy—it's just an implicit policy. Instead of stating explicitly that "a certain number of illegal immigrants can stay," we simply shirk on enforcement efforts. I'm not implying that the people whose job it is to capture illegal immigrants are all sitting around in donut shops ignoring their responsibilities. I'm sure this isn't the case. What I am implying is that if illegal immigration were more important to the United States, we could allocate more resources to solving the problem. By limiting

---

[13] Note that as of 1875, only the federal government has the jurisdiction to remove unauthorized aliens. The Arizona bill of 2010 essentially considers it trespassing to be in the state of Arizona if you are an unlawful alien.

the number of resources, we are limiting our effort—and "allowing" a certain number of illegal immigrants to successfully stay here.

For example, a person usually does not have to provide proof of legal status to obtain a state-issued identification card or driver's license. So, if an illegal immigrant is pulled over for a traffic stop (this is usually my only contact with law enforcement), the officer has no idea that the person is in this country illegally. We could easily change this process, requiring proof of citizenship or legal status for the license, thereby empowering the police officer to identify and penalize the illegal immigrant, but we choose not to. It is important that you realize this is a policy choice, based on the costs and benefits present. Bear in mind, the costs of implicitly allowing some illegal immigration can be large—perhaps larger than the cost of preventing it. (This is what fuels the debate.) As the following article shows, some of these costs are left to non-government entities.

Policing Illegal Hires Puts Some Employers in a Bind

By Miriam Jordan
Wall Street Journal, July 15, 2010

Even as the Obama administration cracks down on companies that hire illegal immigrants, it is simultaneously going after employers that it says go too far in vetting job applicants to ensure they are entitled to work in the U.S.

The Department of Homeland Security currently is auditing employment records of many companies suspected of hiring undocumented workers. Yet in an emerging paradox for businesses, the Justice Department and other agencies have stepped up probes of employers—including restaurant groups, factories and retailers—for allegedly violating anti-discrimination laws by demanding too many identity documents from applicants who aren't U.S. citizens.

To fend off lawsuits or enforcement actions, several companies have recently reached out-of-court settlements with the government; in some instances they paid fines.

"The message is: Employers beware. You need to worry just as much about asking for too many immigration documents as you do about not asking for enough," said Stephen Yale-Loehr, an immigration-law scholar at Cornell University.

The current tension arose from provisions in the federal Immigration Reform and Control Act of 1986 and the Immigration and Nationality Act. The IRCA prohibits employers from knowingly or intentionally hiring illegal immigrants; companies must verify a person's work eligibility through the "I-9" form process, in which new hires present identity documents and employers examine them for authenticity.

Anti-discrimination protections in the INA, meanwhile, guarantee "all individuals authorized to work in the U.S. have the right to seek employment without the added burden of special rules or document demands based on their citizenship status or national origin," said Thomas E. Perez, assistant attorney general for civil rights. He said his unit is prioritizing enforcement of the INA provision.

"The monkey is on the back of employers to make the call," said Mary Pivec, a Washington, D.C., attorney who is defending several companies with immigration-related problems. "We have more enforcement paired with insufficient and inconsistent guidance. Companies are in the crossfire."

By the end of 2010, the Justice Department will have boosted by 25% the total number of attorneys and investigators in its Office of Special Counsel for Immigration-related Unfair Employment Practices. The department doesn't disclose how many companies it is investigating, but a spokesperson didn't deny claims by immigration attorneys that there has been a surge in cases.

"The Obama administration has been much more active in enforcing the immigration law's anti-discrimination provisions than the Bush administration," Mr. Yale-Loehr said.

Companies face a maximum $1,100 civil monetary penalty for each individual from whom they demanded too many documents to prove work eligibility.

"It's a Catch-22," said Randy Johnson, senior vice president for labor and immigration at the U.S. Chamber of Commerce, big business trade group. "Innocent employers get caught up in this snare of enforcement."

Businesses also face a proliferation of state laws designed to punish employers that hire undocumented immigrants. The U.S. Supreme Court is to consider this fall whether Arizona had the right to enact a 2007 law that empowers the state to revoke the business license of any employer found to knowingly hire illegal workers. The court is to determine whether federal immigration law preempts the state's statute.

On July 8, the Justice Department sued Garland Sales Inc., a rug manufacturer in Dalton, Ga., alleging it "engaged in a pattern of bias by imposing unnecessary and discriminatory hurdles" to employment for foreigners who were authorized to work in the U.S. according to a statement by the agency.

The government alleges that Garland required all non-U.S. citizens applying for jobs to present additional documents, in violation of the law. The Justice Department also said Garland "retaliated" against a naturalized U.S. citizen who has limited English skills by rescinding his job offer after he failed to produce a green card, which proves lawful U.S. residency for non-citizens. The person had presented a Social Security card and driver's license.

The company, which employs 300 people, denied the accusations and said it will defend itself.

"Garland Sales does not discriminate against individuals because of race, color, religion, sex, or national origin in its hiring process and categorically denies the allegations," the rug maker said in a news release.

In late June, the Justice Department announced it had reached an agreement with Morton's Restaurant Group Inc. to settle allegations that an outlet in Portland, Ore., had required two noncitizens authorized to work in the U.S. to present more documents than legally required to establish their work eligibility. Both were fired after working for a time while the company reviewed their documentation.

"Morton's fired the workers after it rejected their valid Social Security card and demanded to see additional documentation establishing their work authorization. In contrast, Morton's routinely permitted U.S. citizens to present their Social Security cards for this purpose," according to a Justice Department statement.

Under terms of the out-of-court settlement, Morton's agreed to provide full back pay of $2,880 and $5,715.62 to the employees, pay a $2,200 civil penalty and train Morton's employees in Portland on federal protections for workers against citizenship status and national-origin discrimination. Morton's also agreed to properly train employees nationwide who have any role in evaluating someone's work eligibility.

Roger Drake, communications chief for Morton's, declined to comment on the case.

Some acceptable documents for:
- Establishing Identity:
  - Driver's license or state-issued ID
  - ID card issued by federal, state or local entities
  - School ID card with photo
  - Voter-registration card
- Authorizing Employment:
  - U.S. Social Security card
  - Birth certificate
  - U.S. citizen-identification card
  - Identification card for use of resident citizen in the U.S.
- Acceptable for Either:
  - U.S. passport
  - Permanent-resident or alien-registration receipt card

Source: Department of Homeland Security

Figure 2.5

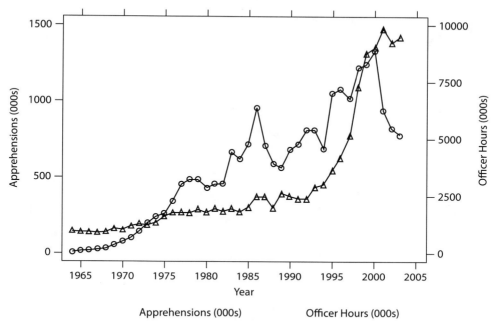

Linewatch Apprehensions and Enforcement by the U.S. Border Patrol

We might be able to get a better understanding of the costs and benefits of limiting the number of illegal entries if we consider the number of apprehensions per unit of effort by border enforcement. Figure 2.5, above, does just this.

The first thing to notice here is that there is an increase in both officer hours (measured on the right-hand-side vertical axis) and the number of apprehensions (measured on the left-hand-side vertical axis). So at least the obvious—having more officers leads to more apprehensions—holds true. Areas where there is some separation between the two trends are interesting. For example, between 1975 and 1995, it appears that the number of hours worked remained relatively constant while the number of apprehensions jumped considerably. There are only a couple of plausible explanations: either border patrol became more efficient for some reason (maybe they developed some new technology like night-vision goggles or unmanned flying drones), or there was a jump in the number of attempts.[14] If the latter is the case, and we assume that the success rate was constant, then it follows that the number of successes by potential immigrants was also greater during that period. As such, the number of illegal immigrants in the United States must have jumped during that period—and we now have another way

---

[14] I suppose it is also possible that would-be illegal immigrants became dumber and less efficient at crossing the border, but I don't see why this would be the case.

Figure 2.6

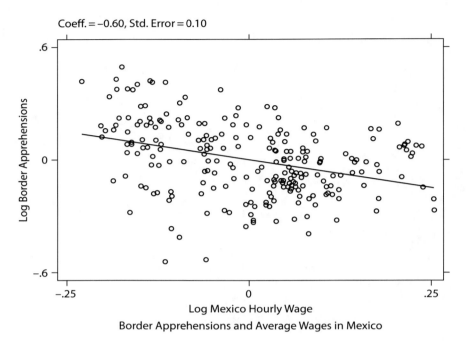

Coeff. = −0.60, Std. Error = 0.10

Border Apprehensions and Average Wages in Mexico

Figure 2.7

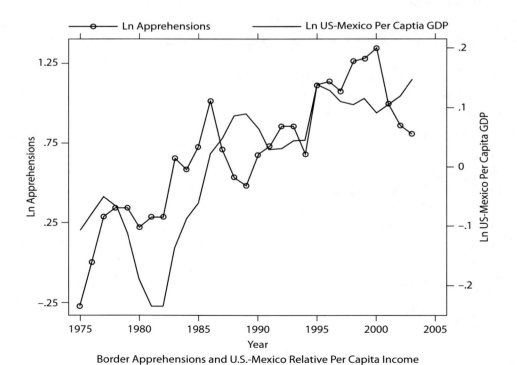

Border Apprehensions and U.S.-Mexico Relative Per Capita Income

of estimating the number of illegal immigrants in the United States—by using the number of apprehensions as a proxy.

Please keep in mind the fact that this figure shows border line apprehensions—the number of people caught in the act of entering the United States illegally. It does not show the number of illegal immigrant apprehensions. The difference is big especially in terms of policy implications. A big fence will not eliminate illegal immigration!

In addition to effort, what else might influence the number of apprehensions? Obviously the number of attempts, but why would that number fluctuate over time? We might expect to see a steady decline in the number of attempts as all of the people interested in migrating eventually succeed, or we might see a relatively steady increase of attempted border crossings as the population grows. Why sudden peaks and valleys? There is one plausible explanation that is somewhat obvious—the value of immigrating must change over time. Consider Figure 2.6, which shows the relationship between the number of border apprehensions (and thus, implicitly, the number of crossings) and the hourly wage in Mexico.

What does the trend line imply? (Notice the slope of the trend line is -0.60.) As the wage in Mexico increases, there are fewer border apprehensions. This seems obvious—a person in Mexico who is just on the fence between migrating to the United States and staying in Mexico (no pun intended) will decide to stay if the wage in Mexico improves. Likewise, as the Mexican wage falls, opportunity in the United States becomes more appealing, assuming the wage in the United States doesn't simultaneously fall. Figure 2.7 provides some additional support for this idea, and provides a nice transition into the next section. It shows the relationship between border apprehensions and the ratio of United States to Mexican GDP per capita.

As you can see, as the ratio of United States to Mexican GDP per capita increases (meaning the United States is becoming relatively richer per person), the number of border apprehensions also increases. (See the *Wall Street Journal* article on page 52.) This shouldn't be shocking to you. I think it's well understood that immigration is driven, at least in part, by the search for economic opportunity. The United States is even called "The Land of Opportunity." However, it is not true that people will always migrate to countries or locations where the wage rate is highest. This may seem counterintuitive at the moment, and requires some explanation. Enter Chapter 3.

With Jobs in U.S. Scarce, Illegal Immigration Slides

By Miriam Jordan
Wall Street Journal, September 5, 2010

Illegal immigration to the U.S. has slowed sharply since 2007, with the bleak U.S. job market apparently discouraging people from heading north.

The influx of illegal immigrants plunged to an estimated 300,000 annually between March 2007 and 2009, from 850,000 a year between March 2000 and March 2005, according to new study released Wednesday by the Pew Hispanic Center, a nonpartisan research group.

The decline contributed to a contraction in the overall size of the undocumented population to 11 million people in March 2009 from a peak of 12 million two years earlier, according to the Pew analysis, which is based on data from the Census Bureau.

All told, illegal immigrants in 2009 represented 28% of the foreign-born population in the U.S. Nearly half of them arrived since 2000, according to Pew.

The latest findings come as the first of hundreds of National Guardsmen began arriving in Arizona this week following authorization from the Obama administration. And Homeland Security Secretary Janet Napolitano announced Monday that the number of drones flying surveillance on the southern border would double by Jan. 1. The increased security has driven up the cost of border crossings, contributing to the drop in illegal entries.

The Pew study found that the flow of Mexicans, who represent 60% of all illegal immigrants in the U.S. plummeted to 150,000 annually during the 2007–2009

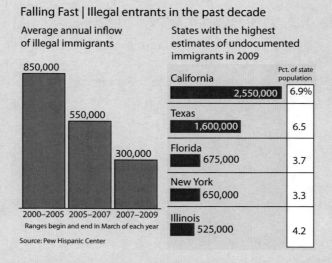

Falling Fast | Illegal entrants in the past decade

Average annual inflow of illegal immigrants

850,000
550,000
300,000

2000–2005   2005–2007   2007–2009
Ranges begin and end in March of each year

Source: Pew Hispanic Center

States with the highest estimates of undocumented immigrants in 2009

	Pct. of state population
California 2,550,000	6.9%
Texas 1,600,000	6.5
Florida 675,000	3.7
New York 650,000	3.3
Illinois 525,000	4.2

period, compared with the annual average of 500,000 during the first half of the decade.

"Not only do we see flows down; it's a steady downward trend in the last four years," said the study's lead author, said Pew demographer Jeffrey Passel.

Mr. Passel, who previously worked at the Census Bureau, said the methodology he developed for calculating the illegal immigrant population is now used by the Department of Homeland Security. He arrived at his estimates using data on the foreign-born population in the Census's Current Population Survey and statistics from DHS on the number of legal immigrants admitted to the U.S.

The mortgage crisis and ensuing economic slump have slashed jobs in construction, tourism and other sectors that are the mainstay for low-skilled Latin Americans. Immigrants already in the U.S. are struggling, and word of their hardship is dissuading those back home from flocking to the U.S.

"People don't want to come now; they know the economy is bad," said Braulio Gonzalez from Guatemala, who has been scraping by as a day laborer outside Los Angeles.

The decrease in the flow of illegal immigrants reported by Pew is supported by new studies from Wayne Cornelius, co-director of the migration-research center at the migration-research center at the University of California, San Diego.

In 2009, the center found that potential migrants in Mexico were "two times less likely" to plan a move to the U.S. than in the pre-recession year of 2006. Among those already in the U.S., more than half said they had experienced a cut in work hours, according to the field research.

Ms. Napolitano noted earlier this week that Washington has dedicated unprecedented man-power and technology to combat illegal immigration. As a result, she said, the influx of undocumented immigrants was falling.

Mr. Cornelius and other experts said the business cycle, not tighter border security, has played the biggest role in the drop in illegal entrants.

"The intensity of U.S. border enforcement has continued to increase during the recession but only gradually," said Mr. Cornelius. "What has changed drastically is the demand for Mexican labor in the U.S. economy."

Mr. Cornelius's research team found no evidence that border fortifications were keeping illegal migrants out of the U.S.: More than nine out of 10 succeed at sneaking into the country eventually, he said.

However, border enforcement has created greater demand for "coyotes," people who smuggle illegal immigrants across the border and transport them to a U.S. destination. Coyote fees have increased in tandem with bolstered enforcement.

Mexicans currently pay about $3,000 to cross the U.S.–Mexico border, compared with $700 in the early 1990s. The cost for immigrants from Central and

South America can top $10,000, which they usually pay in installments after getting jobs in the U.S.

"Because the return on their investment to gain access to the U.S. labor market now looks much less certain, many potential migrants are postponing journeys until the economy grows again," Mr. Cornelius said.

Illegal immigrants represented 5% of the U.S. labor force last year, according to Pew. States where the housing market has been hardest hit saw the steepest decreases in their undocumented population.

The South Atlantic region, stretching from Delaware to Florida, showed significant drops. These states have been deemed new magnets for illegal immigrants, who began to bypass traditional gateway states in the 1990s, such as California and Texas, in search of opportunity further East.

President Barack Obama has asked Congress to send him legislation to create a pathway to citizenship for many illegal immigrants, as well as to further secure borders. Congressional Democrats had talked about moving forward earlier this year, but the matter is widely considered dead for now.

Chapter 3

Why Migrate?

As a resident of the United States, you may think it natural that people want to immigrate, but the details of this decision may be more intricate and complicated than you may think. Start by trying to answer this simple question: why do people migrate? (The text focuses primarily on international migration, but essentially the same analysis applies to any form of labor mobility.) Do people move to find a better job? Maybe, but that can't be the entire story. If I told you that your dream job was available at a terrific wage in Siberia, would you immediately pack up and head there? Unlikely. So, what stops you? Maybe you would miss your family or your dog. Maybe it's too expensive to ship your things around the world. Maybe you don't like cold weather, or the prospect of learning to speak Russian is overwhelming for you. Whatever the reason, your choice to not migrate despite the job offer implies that the cost to you, whether explicit or implicit, outweighs the benefit of the new job.

Why Do People Migrate?

Obviously availability of good jobs alone cannot explain labor migration, but it does in fact play a large part in people's decision to relocate. In general, we can make the following statements about labor mobility[1]:

1. An improvement in the economic opportunities available in the destination increases the net gains to migration and raises the likelihood that the worker moves.
2. An improvement in the economic opportunities at the current region of residence decreases the net gains to migration and lowers the probability that the worker moves.
3. An increase in migration costs lowers the net gains to migration and reduces the likelihood of a move.

Cost of relocating can include the actually monetary burden of travel, the agony of filling out immigration paperwork (if you choose to migrate legally), the opportunity cost of leaving your hometown, or even the possibility of apprehension if you choose to migrate illegally. The complexity of these costs can make analysis of migration decisions less than obvious.

---

[1] Borjas, George, "Labor Economics," ch. 9.

One interesting explicit cost that pertains almost exclusively to immigrants traveling from Mexico to the United States illegally is the expense of hiring a fancy, frequently armored tour guide called a "coyote." These coyotes will usher illegal migrants through the desert that separates the United States and Mexico, and they will even help facilitate transport within the United States upon arrival. (The details of how this system works can be a bit gruesome. Needless to say, people in illegal industries tend to be less than upstanding and they can be downright nasty to their customers.) It is estimated that a typical coyote will cost around $2,000—which is approximately one-third of per capita GDP in Mexico. However, given the prevailing wage differential between the United States and Mexico ($5 to $7 an hour higher in the United States), this fee can be recovered in a matter of weeks.

However, not all costs are explicit. In fact, as we will show here, the majority of migration costs may be implicit (and thus difficult to account for). Consider the illegal immigrants coming from Mexico to the United States by way of coyote services. When they arrive, they face a discriminatory employment environment: employers are frequently not willing to hire anybody without legal status. This implies a reduction in both the number of opportunities for the immigrant and a reduction in expected wage. Also, the ease of consuming public goods like unemployment and welfare is reduced for these people. There is also the treat of capture, which may be psychologically costly for some. All of these are examples of implicit costs, and this list is nowhere near complete.

To illustrate the importance of the implicit cost in migration decisions, consider an example where the only two "countries" are the United States and Puerto Rico. In this case, there is no restriction on movement from one to the other, since both are part of the United States.[2] Thus, the only costs would be the explicit cost of travel and the implicit cost of leaving your hometown. The average wage in the upper United States is $49,000, while in Puerto Rico the average worker earns only $18,000. Certainly the cost of moving from one to the other is less than $31,000. (At the time of writing this, airfare from San Juan to Chicago was $250 per person.) Then why don't we see more movement to the upper United States from Puerto Rico? We must conclude that the implicit costs are too great.

The punch line to this example is this: in equilibrium, even in the long run, we should expect to see wage differentials existing between countries or regions. The idea that eventually the United States and Mexico will have identical prevailing wages in the absence of limited immigration is false. This can be seen within the United States as well—salaries in San Diego, California are higher than they are in

---

[2] As of 1917, people born in Puerto Rico are United States citizens. However, they cannot vote in federal elections unless they become residents of a state (or the District of Columbia). So if you move to Puerto Rico, you can no longer vote even if you are a citizen. You still have to pay federal taxes.

Billings, Montana. So, if the wage in location A is greater than the wage in location B, people may still stay in location B. People do not always migrate to the place with the highest wage.

Present Value Calculation

Let's formalize this a bit. Let w^A be the wage a particular worker can earn in location A, and w^B is the wage for that person in location B. Notice that these wages are functions of things like how skilled the worker is, what their profession is, et cetera. Workers obviously won't make relocation decisions based entirely on today's wage—they will also factor in the value of all future wages, too. So if today is time t (you can think of "today" as a day, or a year, or any arbitrary period of time), then a worker in location A receives w_t^A today and w_{t+1}^A tomorrow, and so on. However, w_{t+1}^A is worth only $\frac{w_{t+1}^A}{1+r}$ today, where r is the rate of interest. The present value calculation adjusts for the fact that you would be willing to accept slightly less than $1 today in exchange for $1 tomorrow. The intuition is simple: if I can put $0.90 in the bank today and let it collect interest so that it grows to be $1 by tomorrow, then $0.90 today and $1 tomorrow are worth the same. If you've ever borrowed money, whether from your credit card or for student loans, you have somehow made this calculation in your mind. Making a similar adjustment for each period's wage, from today until the day the worker retires T periods from now, we get the following present value:

$$PV^A = w_t^A + \frac{w_{t+1}^A}{1+r} + \frac{w_{t+2}^A}{(1+r)^2} + \dots + \frac{w_{t+T}^A}{(1+r)^T}$$

A similar calculation holds for location B. If we assume the T is a sufficiently long period of time (approaching infinity let's say), and that wages are steady over time, we can write this present value as

$$PV^A = \frac{(1+r)}{r}w^A$$

Here's how the math works: start with the infinite sum

$$PV^A = w^A + \frac{w^A}{1+r} + \frac{w^A}{(1+r)^2} + \dots$$

Take out w^A so we have

$$PV^A = w^A\left(1 + \frac{1}{1+r} + \frac{1}{(1+r)^2} + \dots\right)$$

Now focus only on the stuff inside of the parentheses. Let's call this θ, so $PV^A = w^A\theta$ when

$$\theta = 1 + \frac{1}{1+r} + \frac{1}{(1+r)^2} + \dots$$

Rewrite this as

$$\theta = 1 + \frac{1}{1+r}\left[1 + \frac{1}{(1+r)} + \frac{1}{(1+r)^2}\cdots\right] = 1 + \frac{1}{1+r}[\theta]$$

Using the far-left and far-right terms, we have

$$\theta = 1 + \frac{1}{1+r}[\theta]$$

$$\theta - \frac{1}{1+r}[\theta] = 1$$

$$\theta\left(1 - \frac{1}{1+r}\right) = 1$$

Now multiply both sides by $(1 + r)$

$$\theta(1 + r - 1) = 1 + r$$

$$\theta = \frac{1+r}{r}$$

And we get our result that

$$PV^A = w^A \theta = w^A \frac{1+r}{r}$$

Technically, the interest rate should indexed by location also, since it's possible (and likely) that different countries have different rates of interest. For the time being, let's just assume that all locations have the same rate of interest. Either way, a person will migrate from A to B whenever the present value of living in B is greater than the present value of living in A, minus the cost of moving; i.e., a person will move if $\triangle PV = PV^B - PV^A - C > 0$, where C is the cost of moving, both explicit and implicit.

Let's revisit the example of a person considering relocating from Puerto Rico to the upper United States. Rewrite the two equations above, letting Puerto Rico be location A and the United States be location B, to get the following, which characterizes when a person will move from Puerto Rico to the upper United States:

$$\frac{(1+r)}{r}w^{US} - \frac{(1+r)}{r}w^{PR} - C > 0$$

Rearrange to get

$$\frac{(1+r)}{r}(w^{US} - w^{PR}) > C$$

and divide both sides of the inequality by the wage in Puerto Rico to get

$$\frac{(1+r)}{r}\frac{w^{US} - w^{PR}}{w^{PR}} > \frac{C}{w^{PR}}$$

Assuming the interest rate is the same in both locations, and using the average wages of \$49,000 and \$18,000 as stated earlier, the ratio $(w^{US} - w^{PR})/w^{PR} = 1.72$, implying that a person could expect a increase in wage that is equal to 172% of their current wage in Puerto Rico. Assume the interest rate is 5%, so r = .05. In this case, the left-hand side of the equation above is equal to approximately 19.3. In other words, a person would be willing to move from Puerto Rico to the upper United States as long as the cost of relocating C is less than 19.3 times their current Puerto Rican salary of \$18,000. That means the cost of moving must exceed \$347,000 for those remaining in Puerto Rico.

This example really underscores the importance of implicit costs in migration decisions. The value of being near one's home is apparently worth some \$347,000 to the average Puerto Rican. Keep in mind, this example eliminated many of the costs typically involved in international immigration decisions: the immigration process itself was sidestepped since a Puerto Rican can travel freely within the United States without a single page of paperwork.

Why Families Migrate

The decision to migrate will obviously be affected by the presence of family members who will be moving with you. For simplicity, we will assume that a married couple, both of whom work, is debating migration.[3] Keep in mind the analysis that follows is not gender specific, nor does the couple need to be married, et cetera.

Extending the results from the previous section, we can conclude that the couple will move if the sum of their discounted net benefits from moving is positive. That is, letting $\Delta PV_{husband}$ be the change in present value for the man and ΔPV_{wife} be the change in present value for the woman, the couple would choose to relocate if

$$\Delta PV_{husband} + \Delta PV_{wife} > 0.$$

This sum implies that the husband would be willing to accept a \$10,000 reduction in the present value of his earnings and still move as long as the wife receives at least a \$10,001 increase in her present value after the move. Likewise, the wife will be willing to move, despite a loss to her, as long as the husband's gain outweighs her loss. Thus, we see that it is possible for the couple to move even though one of the two expects higher lifetime earnings in their home country. Keep in mind that these calculations include cost of moving.

We can illustrate this result graphically as well. Let the benefit to the wife be measured on the x-axis, and the benefit to the husband be measured on the y-axis. Thus, if the husband expects greater lifetime earnings in present value after the move, he would

---

[3] Much of this section is taken from Borjas, ch. 9.

be north of the origin. Likewise, if the wife would gain from moving, she is east of the origin. So, if the couple were not married, the man would migrate for all points above the x-axis and the woman would migrate for all points to the right of the y-axis.

However, the couple *is* married. So we need to locate points that the two find beneficial as a couple. Rearrange the equation above to get following condition that, if satisfied, will result in the couple's migrating:

$$\Delta PV_{husband} > -\Delta PV_{wife}$$

This is merely the equation for a line in the familiar form $y = mx + b$, where y is $\Delta PV_{husband}$, m is -1, x is ΔPV_{wife}, and b is zero. Since we have replaced the equal sign with > in this equation, we see that the couple will move for any point *above* the line that has slope of -1 and a y-intercept of zero. This is illustrated in the figure below.

There are several areas labeled A through F. Points in area A represent those where, if unmarried, the man would move but the woman would stay. However, since this

Figure 3.1

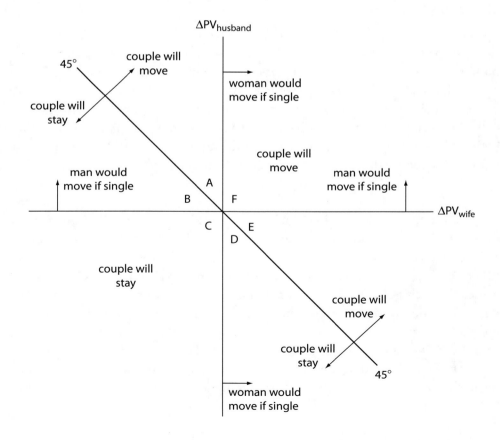

area lies above the 45-degree line, the couple moves. Thus, being married changed the optimal decision for the woman. In this case, we say that the woman is a *tied-mover* since the only reason for her move was the tie of marriage. The same is true about the husband for points in area E; that is the husband is a tied-mover in that region. Points in the area labeled B are those where the man would move if single, and the woman would stay if single, and the couple stays. Thus, the tie of marriage changed the decision for the husband, so we call him a *tied-stayer*. The same is true for the wife in area D: she is the tied-stayer. Points in area F are those where the couple moves and each individual would move if single, so marriage is a non-factor. Likewise for points in area C—the two would stay, married or single.

These calculations may seem like a bit of unrealistic theory to you. While you may have a point—these calculations are probably too complicated for the average potential immigrant—the logic behind present value calculation is definitely on the mind of any immigrant. To consider the question "Am I better off here or there in the long run?" requires no formal mathematical background.

Tough Irish Economy Turns Migration Influx to Exodus

By Guy Chazan and Ainsley Thomson
Wall Street Journal, January 21, 2011

Dublin—Ireland is facing a wave of emigration on a scale unseen since the 1980s, as young people desperate for work turn their backs on an economy ravaged by debt crises, high unemployment and tough austerity measures.

A new report by the Economic and Social Research Institute, a leading Dublin-based think tank, said 100,000 people were expected to leave Ireland from April 2010 to April 2012. That averages out to roughly 1,000 a week or more than 2% of the population.

They are being driven away by a lack of jobs. Ireland's unemployment rate stood at 13.5% last year—about double the rate in Germany—and is expected to remain stubbornly high as the country struggles with sluggish growth and a mountain of public and private debt.

The Irish government has been looking to exports to drive a recovery. Exports have grown strongly; but that appears to have had little effect on the jobless rate. "The problem is that the export part of the economy is not employment-intensive," said Alan Barrett, co-author of ESRI's quarterly economic commentary and an expert in migration.

Danny O'Connor, a 21-year-old trainee carpenter from the southwestern town of Cork, is part of the exodus. He is halfway through an apprenticeship, but

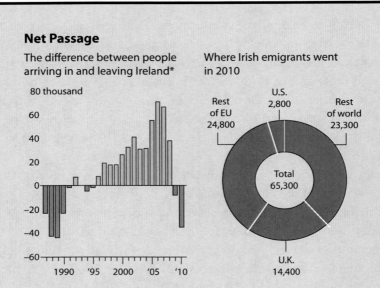

Net Passage

The difference between people arriving in and leaving Ireland*

Where Irish emigrants went in 2010

is already packing his bags for Australia to join a friend who moved there a few months ago and "is loving it."

"There are more opportunities there," he said, while Ireland is likely to be depressed for years to come, with jobs few and far between. "The economy is going to get a lot worse before it gets better," he added.

The new figures mean emigration is likely to be a key issue in Ireland's general-election campaign. On Thursday, Prime Minister Brian Cowen, called new elections for March 11.

"The return of mass emigration is the stark legacy of a tired Fianna Fail-led government on the way out of office," said Joan Burton, finance spokeswoman and deputy leader of the opposition Labour Party.

The migration statistics offer confirmation that the era of the Celtic Tiger is over. During the boom years of the past decade, when the Irish economy was the fastest-growing in Europe, many of the Irish diaspora headed home to share in the country's newfound prosperity. Poles, Slovaks and other Eastern Europeans also piled in to seek work in Ireland's thriving construction sector.

But hopes of a sustained revival were dashed by last year's banking crisis, which climaxed when Ireland was forced to accept a rescue package from the European Union and International Monetary Fund.

Ireland has experienced several waves of high emigration in its history, often in response to calamities both natural and man-made. During the Irish Potato Famine of the mid-19th century, which according to some estimates killed a million people, one million more emigrated from Ireland. At the height of the famine, at least

200,000 people a year were leaving, most of them to the U.S., Canada, Australia and the U.K.

In the 1950s, thousands of laborers and semiskilled workers left Ireland for the U.K., then in the grip of a road-building boom. In the 1980s, with unemployment running at 15%, public finances in disarray and the economy stagnating, some 200,000 emigrated. "Unlike in the 1950s, many of these were well-educated and highly-skilled," says Dr. Barrett. That wave peaked in 1989, when 44,000 left Ireland, according to ESRI.

Emigration began to tick up again in the postboom period, with 35,000 leaving from April 2006 to April 2010. ESRI said 60% of these were non-nationals—migrants returning home—and 40% indigenous Irish.

The main destination for those leaving Ireland in 2010 was the U.K., which absorbed some 14,000 Irish immigrants. The next most-popular destinations were the newer EU member states, including Poland and the Czech Republic. EU members France and Germany came in third. Some 23,000 went to other countries, including Australia and New Zealand, and a modest 2,800 moved to the U.S., according to figures from Ireland's Central Statistics Office.

A More Sophisticated Model of Why People Migrate

With a little background in econometrics (see pages 13 to 17), we can make considerable strides toward a more sophisticated—and more empirically testable—model of immigration. One such model has been called the "gravity model" of immigration[1], thanks to its similarity (in appearance and intuition) to Newton's equation for the force of gravity between two masses (m and M) separated by some distance (r). In *The Principia*, the equation is

$$Force = G\,\frac{mM}{r^2}$$

where G is a very small constant ($6.67 \cdot 10^{-11}$). Here, we interpret the "force" to be the tendency for migration to occur between two locations (i and j). Instead of mass for

---

[1]   See Bodvarsson, Orn, and H. Van den Berg, "The Economics of Immigration," Springer (2009) for example, p. 62.

each, we substitute GDP and we of course lose the gravitational constant G. The result is

$$Immigration = \frac{GDP_i \cdot GDP_j}{r^2}$$

and the interpretation of r is still the distance between the two objects.[2] If you remember the properties of logarithms well enough, you will see that we can eliminate the fraction by taking the natural log of both sides, to get

$$\ln(Immigration) = ln(GDP_i \cdot GDP_j) - ln(r^2)$$

We can use this as a linear regression model, simply by adding an intercept, a coefficient for each term and the error term, as shown below.

$$\ln(Immigration_{ij}) = \beta_0 + \beta_1 ln(GDP_i \cdot GDP_j) + \beta_2 ln(r^2) + u$$

The subscript on "Immigration" is designed to indicate that movement is from location i to location j.

We have now completed step #1 from page 14 on how to develop an empirical model. Step #2 tells us to determine what our economic theory predicts about the coefficients. Keeping the physics part of our brain awake for another second or two, you should hopefully realize that the greater the mass of the objects (the greater the GDPs), the stronger the gravitational force between the two (the greater the immigration tendency between the locations). Thus, we would expect the sign of β_1 to be positive. As distance increases, the force (of gravity and migration) should decrease, so the sign of β_2 should be negative. (That's where the negative sign went—I didn't make a mistake. It's conventional to write the regression model with all plus signs and then predict that the coefficient is negative instead of assuming all coefficients are positive and using some minus signs.)

There are several changes and additions that may be tempting at this point. We obviously have not accounted for all possible factors that affect migration decisions. For example, we have not included a variable that directly addresses the population of either country. It seems likely more population would lead to more migration. We also may want to include a variable to estimate the effect of the current stock of immigrants in the destination country. Would you be more willing to migrate to Hungary if there were other Americans around, or would you rather be the only one there? Probably

---

[2] I'm not sure that the economic equivalent of center of mass is as important here as it is in physics. If it were, and we used GDP for various cities as mass, then the center of mass for the United States would probably be somewhere in Arkansas. I don't think many people really want to migrate there, a notion that is supported empirically.

the former is the case. It also may make sense to use some measurement of *relative* incomes instead of *absolute* incomes in each country. This is similar to what we did in the previous sections. Other variables might be some indicator for whether the countries share a border, share a language, or share other cultural things that would make the transition for an immigrant easier (for example, a German migrating to Switzerland may have an easier time than a German migrating to Denmark or Sweden, even though the distance to each is the same). Including all of these things would give a model that looks something like this:

$$\ln(Immigration_{ij}) = \beta_0 + \beta_1 ln\left(\frac{GDP_j}{GDP_i}\right) + \beta_2 ln(Cost_{ij}) + \beta_3 ln(Pop_i) + \sum_{n=4}^{N} \beta_n X_n + u$$

where $Cost_{ij}$ is for cost of migrating from i to j (I replace distance with something more general—cost, but please recognize that distance and cost are related!), Pop_i is obviously population (here I included only the population of the origin country—you may want to include the population of the destination, too) and X_n is any other variable describing properties and characteristics of either country like those mentioned above (there can be a ton of these or none at all—it's up to you as the person modeling this).

From here, as a researcher, you follow step #3 on page 14—collect data. This has been done with models very similar to the one above by many researchers. Most of their results conclude the same two things: β_1 is positive and β_2 is negative. You shouldn't think, by the way, that just because people have used similar models before that nothing else needs to be done to understand migration decisions. The value of new research comes from not only the introduction of new variables, but also from new data sources and new techniques. Even small tweaks to the model can add to our general knowledge about the topic.

Chapter 4

Who Migrates?

Demographic Overview

Immigration to the United States was largely dominated by Europeans throughout most of the United States' history until the 1960s and 1970s. Since, the most common region of origin is Latin America; Asia is second; and Europe is now ranked third. How do recent immigrants differ from their predecessors? How do immigrants in general differ from natives? To answer these questions, let's begin with a snapshot of where the United States' immigrants are coming from, which is given in Table 4.1.

Table 4.1[1]

			Source countries of US immigrants, 2003			
	Foreign-born population		**Cohorts by arrival period**			
	Level (thousands)	**Percent of total**	**Pre-1970**	**1970–79**	**1980–89**	**1990–2003**
			Number (thousands)			
All countries	**34,612**	**100.0**	**4,759**	**4,983**	**8,213**	**16,657**
Region of birth			Percent of arrival-period cohort			
Latin America	18,285	52.8	35.33	47.6	56.4	57.6
Asia	8,994	26.0	14.0	33.3	29.3	25.6
Europe	5,415	15.6	40.6	14.6	9.7	11.7
Other areas	1,918	5.5	10.1	4.5	4.6	5.0
Country of birth						
Mexico	10,237	29.6	16.0	26.4	30.1	34.1
Philippines	1,458	4.2	2.9	5.9	4.9	3.7
India	1,184	3.4	0.8	3.5	2.5	4.6
China	1,168	3.4	2.6	3.0	3.1	3.8
Germany	1,091	3.2	12.5	2.6	1.8	1.3
El Salvador	1,025	3.0	0.6	2.0	4.3	3.3
Cuba	1,005	2.9	7.9	2.9	2.2	1.9
Vietnam	947	2.7	0.5	4.5	3.4	2.5
South Korea	916	2.6	1.3	4.1	3.8	2.0
Canada	853	2.5	8.2	2.2	1.4	1.4
Dominican Republic	726	2.1	1.3	2.3	2.3	2.2

Source: March 2003 Current Population Survey.

---

[1] DHS Yearbook of Immigration Statistics: 2009.

Table 4.2[2]

PERSONS OBTAINING LPR STATUS BY REGION

Country of list residence	1990 to 1999	2001	2003	2005	2007	2009
Total	9,775,398	1,058,902	703,542	1,122,257	1,052,415	1,130,818
Europe	1,348,612	169,948	97,186	170,126	109,243	114,992
Austria-Hungary	27,529	2,303	2,176	4,569	2,057	7,555
Austria	18,234	996	1,160	3,002	849	6,260
Hungary	9,295	1,307	1,016	1,567	1,208	1,295
Belgium	7,077	997	515	1,031	733	764
Bulgaria	16,948	4,273	3,706	5,451	3,766	3,015
Czechoslovakia	8,970	1,911	1,472	2,182	1,851	1,649
Denmark	6,189	732	435	714	505	606
Finland	3,970	497	230	549	385	421
France	35,945	5,379	2,926	5,035	3,680	4,882
Germany	92,207	21,992	8,061	12,864	8,640	8,612
Greece	25,403	1,941	900	1,473	1,152	1,076
Ireland	65,384	1,531	1,002	2,083	1,599	1,708
Italy	75,992	3,332	1,890	3,179	2,682	3,143
Netherlands	13,345	1,188	1,321	2,150	1,482	1,695
Norway-Sweden	17,825	2,544	1,516	2,264	1,604	1,726
Norway	5,211	582	385	472	388	429
Sweden	12,614	1,962	1,131	1,792	1,216	1,297
Poland	172,249	12,308	11,004	14,836	9,717	8,384
Portugal	25,497	1,611	808	1,084	1,054	966
Romania	48,136	6,206	3,305	6,431	5,240	4,557
Russia	433,427	21,576	14,267	20,641	11,706	10,362
Spain	18,443	1,875	1,102	2,002	1,810	2,118
Switzerland	11,768	1,786	862	1,465	885	1,015
United Kingdom	156,182	20,118	11,155	21,956	16,113	17,417
Yugoslavia	57,039	21,854	8,270	19,249	6,364	5,992
Other Europe	29,087	33,294	20,263	38,918	26,218	27,329
Asia	2,159,899	343,056	240,699	392,977	370,903	394,874
China	342,058	50,677	37,342	64,887	70,924	60,896
Hong Kong	116,894	10,282	5,015	5,004	4,450	3,389
India	352,528	65,673	47,032	79,139	55,371	54,360
Iran	76,899	8,003	4,696	7,306	8,098	8,840
Israel	41,340	4,892	3,686	6,963	4,999	6,208
Japan	66,582	10,424	6,702	9,929	7,213	8,218
Jordan	42,755	5,106	4,008	5,430	5,516	7,850
Korea (N and S)	179,770	19,728	12,076	26,002	21,278	25,582
Philippines	534,338	50,644	43,133	57,654	68,792	58,107
Syria	22,906	3,542	2,046	3,350	2,550	4,775
Taiwan	132,647	12,457	7,168	9,389	9,053	8,105
Turkey	38,647	3,463	3,318	6,449	4,728	7,943
Vietnam	275,379	34,537	21,227	30,832	27,510	28,397

[2] Hanson, "Why Does Immigration Divide America?" p. 14.

Country of list residence	1990 to 1999	2001	2003	2005	2007	2009
Other Asia	637,116	63,628	43,250	80,643	80,421	112,204
America	5,137,743	470,794	305,936	432,726	434,272	479,845
Canada/Newfoundland	194,788	29,991	16,447	29,930	20,324	22,508
Mexico	2,757,418	204,032	114,758	157,992	143,180	164,067
Caribbean	1,004,687	96,384	67,498	91,371	114,318	144,897
Cuba	159,037	25,832	8,685	20,651	25,441	38,111
Dominican Rupublic	359,818	21,139	26,112	27,365	27,875	49,381
Haiti	177,446	22,470	11,924	13,491	29,978	23,994
Jamaica	177,143	15,031	13,045	17,774	18,873	21,494
Other Caribbean	131,243	11,912	7,732	12,090	12,151	11,917
Central America	610,189	72,504	53,283	52,629	53,834	47,013
Belize	12,600	982	616	901	1,089	1,073
Costa Rica	17,054	1,863	1,322	2,479	2,722	2,552
El Salvador	273,017	30,876	27,854	20,891	20,009	19,342
Guatamala	126,043	13,399	14,195	16,468	17,198	11,881
Honduras	72,880	6,546	4,582	6,825	7,300	6,290
Nigeria	10,446	16,908	3,503	3,196	3,587	4,029
Panama	28,149	1,930	1,211	1,869	1,929	1,846
South America	570,624	67,880	53,946	100,803	102,616	101,359
Argentina	30,065	3,426	3,193	6,945	5,375	5,672
Bolivia	18,111	1,804	1,365	2,164	2,326	2,789
Brazil	50,744	9,391	6,108	16,329	13,546	14,428
Chile	18,200	1,881	1,255	2,354	2,202	2,240
Colombia	137,985	16,234	14,400	24,705	32,055	27,221
Ecuador	81,358	9,654	7,022	11,528	12,011	12,083
Guana	74,407	7,835	6,373	8,771	5,288	6,326
Paraguay	6,082	464	222	523	518	551
Peru	110,117	10,838	9,169	15,205	17,056	16,706
Suriname	2,285	254	175	287	193	214
Uruguay	6,062	516	470	1,110	1,340	1,727
Venezuela	35,180	5,576	4,190	10,870	10,696	11,392
Africa	346,416	50,009	45,559	79,697	89,277	122,804
Egypt	44,604	5,333	3,928	10,296	10,178	10,810
Ethiopia	40,097	4,620	5,969	8,378	11,340	14,674
Liberia	13,587	1,477	1,081	1,846	3,771	3,695
Morocco	15,768	4,752	2,969	4,165	4,311	5,235
South Africa	21,964	4,046	2,088	4,425	2,842	3,175
Other Africa	210,396	29,781	29,524	50,587	56,835	85,215
Oceania	56,800	7,201	5,076	7,432	6,639	6,142
Australia	24,283	3,714	2,488	4,090	3,026	3,098
New Zealand	8,600	1,347	1,030	1,457	1,234	1,127
Other Oceania	23,912	2,140	1,558	1,885	2,379	1,917

As you can see, the percent of foreign-born from Latin America has nearly doubled during the past three decades, while foreign-born from Europe have fallen to nearly a quarter of the previous value for the same period. Mexico and Germany seem to be driving these trends. Keep in mind that the data in Table 4.1 represent an overview of the number of foreign-born, not of legal entries into the United States. This means that illegal immigrants should be included in the numbers in Table 4.1. For completeness, Table 4.2 provides additional data concerning new LPRs by year and region. There is nothing profound in the table that follows, it's primarily just so you can find your favorite country and see how many LPRs arrived recently.

The United States sees more female immigrants than male, with the most popular age at time of arrival being between 25 and 34 years (25 to 29 for women, 30 to 34 for men). This is consistent with migration in search of jobs, since these ages are prime working years. Married couples outnumber single individuals nearly 2 to 1, and "no occupation" (primarily students) is the most common job listed. Of those with jobs outside of the home, "management, professional, and related occupations" tops the list. This is consistent with the United States policy of admitting people with "exceptional" skill. These data are summarized in Table 4.3.

The information in Table 4.3 hints at an interesting and important question: how do the skills of immigrants compare with those of native workers? Notice the high proportion of service occupations and production, transportation, and material moving trades. These low-skill occupations, in addition to unemployed and others not working outside the home, comprise well over half of the new LPRs for this particular year. In fact, depending on what you classify as "high skilled," high-skilled labor represents only 10% of new LPRs in 2009. What are the implications of importing primarily low-skilled labor? Further, do we receive the most-skilled, or the least-skilled workers from the originating nations? For example, is it possible that these workers appear to be low skilled simply because natives are so massively over skilled that all others pale in comparison? This seems unlikely, which implies that we are pulling the people from the lower-skilled portion of the population in the countries that immigrants are coming from. Is this a good idea? It seems plausible that doing so will result in a less-educated, less-skilled population—which certainly doesn't sound good. Shouldn't we want only the best and brightest to come to the United States? Maybe, but maybe not. It's true that we want some high-skilled workers, but can we completely eliminate low-skilled workers? What's the best mix of high and low skills?

Table 4.3

NEW LPRs BY GENDER, AGE, MARITAL STATUS, AND OCCUPATION: FISCAL YEAR 2009

Characteristic	Total	Male	Female
AGE			
Total	1,130,818	513,015	617,799
Under 1 year	5,782	2,706	3,076
1 to 4 years	32,395	15,975	16,420
5 to 9 years	55,373	28,263	27,110
10 to 14 years	75,328	38,720	36,608
15 to 19 years	94,801	48,195	46,606
20 to 24 years	114,881	50,315	64,566
25 to 29 years	136,807	58,445	78,361
30 to 34 years	141,060	65,551	75,509
35 to 39 years	120,813	56,835	63,978
40 to 44 years	90,088	40,562	49,526
45 to 49 years	49,989	29,975	40,012
50 to 54 years	54,632	22,263	32,368
55 to 59 years	44,355	17,132	27,223
60 to 64 years	35,853	13,861	21,992
65 to 74 years	43,873	18,142	25,731
75 years and over	14,786	6,073	8,713
BROAD AGE GROUP			
Total	1,130,818	513,015	617,799
Under 16 years	185,960	94,529	91,431
16 to 20 years	101,864	50,720	51,144
21 years and over	842,992	367,764	475,224
MARITAL STATUS			
Total	1,130,818	513,015	617,799
Single	417,232	219,812	197,419
Married	654,674	279,354	375,320
Widowed	28,439	3,288	25,151
Divorced/separated	26,015	8,261	17,754
Unknown	4,458	2,300	2,155
OCCUPATION			
Total	1,130,818	513,015	617,799
Management, professional and related occupations	107,530	68,097	39,433
Service occupations	60,758	33,801	26,957
Sales and office occupations	40,512	18,221	22,291
Farming, fishing, and forestry occupations	13,609	11,262	2,347
Construction, extraction, maintenance, and repair occupations	8,835	8,666	169
Production, transportation, and material moving occupations	47,815	36,937	10,884
Military	65	47	18
No occupatioin/not working outside home	563,569	197,824	365,744
Homemakers	165,742	4,871	160,871
Students or children	291,460	146,913	144,546
Retirees	10,523	4,857	5,666
Unemployed	95,844	41,183	54,661
Unknown	288,125	138,166	149,956

Who Do We Want To Immigrate?

In 1886, France delivered the Statue of Liberty to the United States as a gift in honor of America's centennial celebration of independence from the British.[3] The statue's relevance to immigration has been profound ever since—not only has it served as the iconic image of the American dream that has beckoned to generation of immigrants, but it also served as the location for the signing of the 1965 Immigration and Nationality Act by President Lyndon Johnson. On a plaque at the base of the Statue of Liberty is a poem by Emma Lazarus called "The New Colossus," which summarizes the philosophy of United States concerning the quality of immigrants we are willing to accept:

> Not like the brazen giant of Greek fame,
> With conquering limbs astride from land to land;
> Here at our sea-washed, sunset gates shall stand
> A mighty woman with a torch, whose flame
> Is the imprisoned lightning, and her name
> Mother of Exiles. From her beacon-hand
> Glows world-wide welcome; her mild eyes command
> The air-bridged harbor that twin cities frame.
> "Keep ancient lands, your storied pomp!" cries she
> With silent lips. ***Give me your tired, your poor,***
> ***Your huddled masses yearning to breathe free,***
> ***The wretched refuse of your teeming shore.***
> ***Send these, the homeless, tempest-tost to me,***
> I lift my lamp beside the golden door!"

The statement "Give me your tired, your poor…" does not necessarily instill a sense of high admission standards. How skilled are the immigrants who come to the United States? Are they "wretched refuse," or are they in fact more educated and skilled than natives? Has this changed over time?

As it turns out, education levels of immigrants upon arrival are similar to that of natives, although there is considerable variation by region. Table 4.4 gives a sample of education levels for immigrant men from various locations. The table also provides average wage by region, a topic that will be discussed in more detail in later chapters.

There are some important things to notice at this point about Table 4.4. Look at the years of schooling for immigrants from most European countries. The average is relatively large—many are even larger than the native 13.2 average. Now look at immigrants from Mexico—only 7.6 years of schooling on average. Although we cannot

---

[3] Thank you Frédéric Bartholdi.

Table 4.4[4]

Education and Wages of Immigrant Men, by Country of Birth, 1990

Country of birth	Years of schooling	Percent wage differential between immigrants and natives	Country of birth	Years of schooling	Percent wage differential between immigrants and natives
Europe			Americas		
Germany	13.9	24.5	Canada	13.8	24.0
Greece	11.8	−0.9	Cuba	11.7	−15.3
Italy	10.9	16.1	Dominican Republic	10.3	−29.2
Poland	12.8	−0.3	El Salvador	8.6	−39.7
Portugal	8.3	−3.1	Haiti	11.2	−30.2
U.S.S.R.	14.2	6.2	Jamaica	12.0	−11.2
United Kingdom	14.6	37.2	Mexico	7.6	−39.5
Asia			Africa		
Cambodia	10.2	−30.8	Egypt	15.6	12.2
China	12.8	−21.3	Ethiopia	14.0	−21.0
India	15.9	17.6	Nigeria	15.8	−18.9
Korea	14.3	−12.0	Australia	15.2	33.0
Laos	10.0	−32.4	Native-born workers	13.2	—
Philippines	14.1	−5.9			
Vietnam	12.3	−18.9			

Source: George J. Borjas, "The Economics of Immigration," *Journal of Economic Literature* 32 (December 1994), p. 1686.

Note: The data refer to salaried men who are twenty-five to sixty-four years old and are employed in the civilian sector.

infer this from these data, let's assume these figures have remained relatively constant over time. If this is indeed the case, what would we expect to see to the average education level of immigrants over time? Well, we know that the United States has seen a shift from primarily European immigrants to Mexican immigrants during the second half of the 20th century. This implies that the average, randomly selected immigrant would have been more educated (and more European) long ago. Are immigrants become less educated over time? Why have we seen this change?

Roy Model[5]

Let's make our analysis more robust. The broad question we are addressing is this: who finds it most beneficial to migrate to the United States, the most skilled/educated or the least skilled/educated? If the United States is the recipient of the most-skilled workers from another country, we say there is a *positive selection* of immigrants (i.e., immigrants are chosen from the right tail of the skill distribution). If the United States receives the lowest-skilled workers from the originating country, then immigrants are negatively selected (immigrants are chosen from the left tail of the skill distribution).

---

[4] Borjas, *Heaven's Door*, p. 43.

[5] This analysis comes originally from Andrew Roy, by way of an application to immigration by George Borjas. See Andrew D. Roy, "Some Thoughts on the Distribution of Earnings," *Oxford Economic Papers*, 3, June 1951, pages 135–146.

Figure 4.1

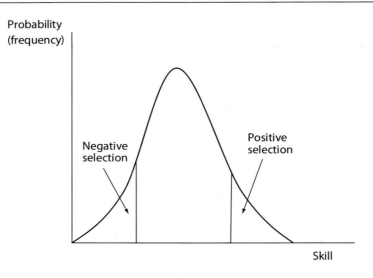

Figure 4.2

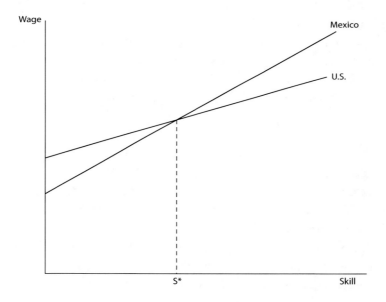

As a potential immigrant with a given set of skills and education, a person will choose to reside in the country that has the highest return to their particular skill level. For example, if you are low-skill, you will choose to live in a country where low-skill workers are paid relatively well. What types of countries treat low-skill workers the best, and which treat low-skill workers the worst? Well, socialist nations or those nations with great income equality will tend to have low-skill workers that are paid a relatively higher wage than countries with poor income equality. By definition, income equality means low-skill or poor workers are paid almost the same as high-skill or rich workers. True, some of this compensation may be in the form of public aid, such as welfare, but this still contributes to the income of low-skilled workers. So if you are low-skill, you should choose to live in a country that has an equal distribution of income. Likewise, if you are high-skilled, you will choose a country that rewards those with high skill the most. Which countries are these? These are the most competitive countries, where equality is less important than performance. Countries that have low income equality—the rich are very rich and the poor are very poor—reward skilled workers the most.

Consider two countries: the United States and Mexico. The United States has a Gini Coefficient of about 0.40 while Mexico's is about 0.46. Thus, income is distributed more equally in the United States than in Mexico. If we were to graph the wage as a function of skill in each of these countries, we would find that the Mexico rewards high-skill workers more than the United States does. Conversely, the United States "rewards" low-skill workers more than Mexico by way of things like minimum wage and transfer payments. We would graph this as shown in Figure 4.2. Notice that both lines must be upward sloping since wage is assumed to increase in skill.

Any worker who has a skill level less than s* will prefer to live in the United States (since the United States' line is higher), and any worker with more skill than s* will prefer to live in Mexico. This means that *workers with less skill will migrate to the United States*, so the United States will be receiving negatively selected immigrants from Mexico.

This result does not mean that all immigrants coming to the United States will be low-skilled. For example, the United States should, by the same logic, import high-skilled immigrants from countries with more income equality (Sweden, for example). Although the Roy Model provides us some foundation for understanding the skills of immigrants, the conclusions you draw from this simple diagram may be inconsistent with what you see in the world. It's a very limited model.

Skill can be difficult to measure, so we may choose to use a proxy like education. The issue is that human capital can consist of things relatively easy to measure like education or job experience, or it can consist of things that are much harder to quantify like knowledge. Even if we're talking about job experience, not all experience will transfer to a new position. So you may have worked 10 years as an engineer, but once you come to the United States you are faced with different regulations, building codes, materials, et cetera, all of which make your experience less than perfectly useful.

Can you think of anything not present in the Roy Model? Does skill affect anything besides expected wage when it comes to migration decisions? What about the cost of immigrating? It seems logical that a person who is highly educated (and thus assumed to be highly skilled) may have a lower cost of immigration than an uneducated person

Figure 4.3

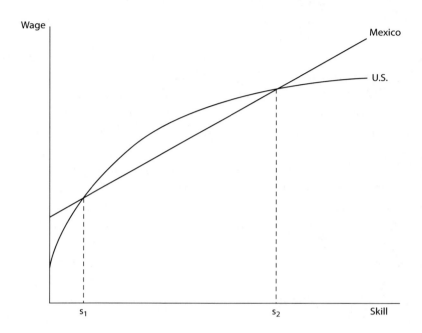

from the same region. To understand this, you need only think about a person's ability to speak a foreign language or understand complicated immigration paperwork. Further, many countries like the United States will encourage people with certain skills to immigrate, so perhaps the costs are lower for high-skill workers thanks to some implicit or explicit policy in the destination country. How would we include the observation that skill affects the cost of immigrating into the Roy Model? The following section addresses this.

A Second Look at the Roy Model

A recent paper by Daniel Chiquiar from the Bank of Mexico and Gordon Hanson at UCSD[6] revisited the Roy Model and took a slightly different approach. Much like Roy and those who followed,[7] Chiquiar and Hanson assumed that wage is an increasing function of education or skill. Let's continue the previous example, and consider a

[6] D. Chiquiar and G.H. Hanson, (2005), "International Migration, Self-Selection, and the Distribution of Wages: Evidence from Mexico and the United States," *Journal of Political Economy*, vol. 113, pp. 239–281.

[7] Borjas, George J. (1987). "Self-Selection and the Earnings of Immigrants," *American Economic Review*, v. 77, n. 4, pp. 531–553.

person who is thinking about migrating from Mexico to the United States. Using this framework, wages in Mexico could be given by the following expression:

$$w_{Mexico} = b_{Mexico} + \delta_{Mexico}s,$$

where w_{Mexico} is the wage in Mexico, b_{Mexico} is some base wage (perhaps minimum wage, but not necessarily), δ_{Mexico} is the incremental return to an additional little bit of schooling or skill, and s is the amount of school/skill. (We will use school and skill interchangeably from now on since the connection between the two is obvious.) Likewise in the destination country, which we will index with "US," we could write wage as the following:

$$w_{US} = b_{US} + \delta_{US}s.$$

Notice that the base wage and the marginal change in wage are different in the two countries. This means that a person with a certain skill level is likely to be paid a different wage in the originating country than they would in the destination country. Notice also that for the United States and Mexico, it is likely that $\delta_{Mexico} > \delta_{US}$ since skill is scarcer in Mexico than in the United States—so the marginal return to skill should be higher in Mexico. This is reflected in the original diagram (in the previous section) by the slope of each country's line. Mexico had a steeper curve since the marginal return to skill was higher. So we see that the variable δ is the slope of function that relates skill to wage.

Everything so far is exactly as it was in the original Roy Model. However, the next step goes in a slightly different direction. The original Roy Model, as applied to immigration literature, assumed a fixed cost of relocating. As we discussed earlier, this cost includes both explicit (the cost of travel, coyotes, hiring somebody to help with paperwork, et cetera) and implicit (the cost of leaving your hometown) costs. However, it seems plausible that the cost of migrating would be a function, at least in part, of a person's level of education. For example, more-educated people may have an easier time understanding the intricacies of immigration law, or they may be better at reading documents that are printed in a foreign language, and so on. Thus, education and cost of migrating should be inversely related.

Specifically, let C be the cost of migrating, and let π denote the number of hours an immigrant would have to work in order to cover the cost C. Logically,

$$\pi = \frac{C}{w_{Mexico}}$$

Using the fact the migration cost is decreasing in education, we could use the following expression for π in terms of skill:

$$\pi = b_{\pi} - \delta_{\pi}s$$

where, as before, b_π is some base cost (in terms of hours) and δ_π is the marginal change in π given a small increase in skill or education. Notice that the minus sign in front of δ_π indicates that δ_π must be positive (we need π to decrease as s increases). In the original Roy Model, δ_π had a value of zero, so the cost of moving for all skill levels was simply b_π. The diagram changes in light of the generalization that cost is a function of skill, as illustrated on page 76. Although we don't explicitly graph the cost function, it does affect the shape of the curves, as seen in Figure 4.3.

For people who have skill levels that fall in the interval between the origin and skill level s_1, the cost of moving is too great (thanks to their low skill level), so they choose to stay in Mexico. Notice that the line for Mexico is above the line for the United States for that region of skill. People with skill levels above s_2 also stay in Mexico, but for a different reason: now it's because the enormous return to high skill in that country eliminates the incentive to migrate. This choice to stay is despite the low cost of moving for this group. People who have skill levels in the interval between s_1 and s_2 are those who will migrate to the United States since the expected wage less the cost of moving for that particular level of skill is higher in the United States than in Mexico (the United States' line is above Mexico's). Thus, if the cost of migration is allowed to vary as a function of skill, we see that the United States will receive workers in the middle of the skill distribution. This is a very different result from the original Roy Model, where the United States received the most unskilled workers.

Here are a few comments and some things to think about. This model, although arguably improved from the original Roy Model, still gives us only a partial picture of the type of people we will see moving from Mexico to the United States (of course this analysis could be extended to any two countries). For example, this model addresses only people who are moving in order to maximize expected wages—in other words this model considers only workers. If we refer back to Table 2.3, over half of the new LPRs listed themselves as having "no occupation." So this model does not apply. Of course, there is a large group of people not represented in the data of Table 2.3 (illegal immigrants) for whom this model does apply since they are workers and are motivated by wage differentials. My point here is that although this model seems to be well developed, it may still not completely describe the demographics of immigrants.

The conclusion that the United States receives the middle-skilled workers is open for interpretation. Are we receiving the middle of the distribution of Mexican skills, or do immigrants fall into the middle of the United States distribution for skill? There is a big difference. The average Mexican receives fewer years of education than the average American. (The poor quality of Mexican schools has been an ongoing concern for our southern neighbors.) As a result, it is safe to say that Mexico's distribution of skill is lower (more precisely, the mean is lower) than the distribution in the United States. This means that the "middle" of the distribution for Mexico is more like the "bottom" of the United States' distribution. (Again, more precisely we would say that a person selected at random in Mexico would have a lower expected education level than a randomly selected person in the United States.) So does the United States receive people from the middle of Mexico's distribution, which implies we are receiving workers who are near the bottom of our distribution? Or is it the case that the United States is importing workers near the middle of the United States' distribution, which implies that Mexico is losing people near the top of their distribution? The model is done here from the perspective of Mexico—it models the thought process of a potential Mexican immigrant. As a result, we should conclude that the former is the case—that the United States is pulling people from the middle of Mexico's distribution (and thus the left tail of the United States'). However, this isn't really clear from the model, and it does point out that a closer comparison of average skill levels (or perhaps average wage levels) is necessary to fully understand migration demographics.

Theory Wage Differentials[8]

The Roy Model and the modified Roy Model of Chiquiar and Hanson provide some insight to the types of skills immigrant workers may possess. Is there any empirical evidence to support these conclusions? The answer is yes, and to show this we turn to the distribution of wages. The mathematics in this section can get a little hairy, but the result is intuitive enough to be useful even if the math mystifies you.[9]

Our goal will be to determine if an immigrant worker would make a high wage or a low wage if they were still working back in their home country. If they would make a low wage, then we can safely conclude that they are low-skill—support for the original Roy Model. If they would make a high wage (or at least a not-low wage), then we can conclude that they are not low-skill—support for the modified Roy Model. Here's the catch: we can never observe an immigrant's wage in their native country since they don't work in their native country anymore. For example, we want to estimate what a Mexican immigrant (who currently lives in the United States) would make if they currently worked in Mexico instead. But since this immigrant doesn't work in Mexico, we cannot observe this wage—instead, we have to estimate it.

I know that some of you are thinking something along these lines: "If I ask an immigrant what they used to do before they migrated (let's say they were a factory worker who makes teddy bears) and then go back to wherever they came from (let's say

---

[8] This section requires a decent understanding of probability theory.

[9] The material in this section is taken from D. Chiquiar and G.H. Hanson, (2005), "International Migration, Self-Selection, and the Distribution of Wages: Evidence from Mexico and the United States," *Journal of Political Economy*, vol. 113, pp. 239–281. I have simplified some of the math, which technically undermines the beauty of the paper slightly, but I think technical details can be overwhelming and exceed the scope of this text.

Figure 4.4

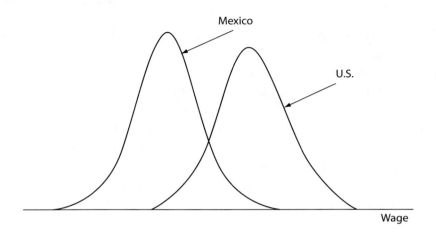

Mexico) and find a person with the same job (teddy bear factory) and ask that person how much they make (let's say $5 an hour after exchange-rate conversion) then I can conclude that the immigrant currently in the United States would be making exactly that amount if they were instead working back in their home country." Unfortunately, this logic doesn't work. You see, the immigrant currently in the United States may have had a job in the teddy bear factory back in Mexico, but you cannot assume they made the same $5 an hour that their replacement makes. When they left for the United States, the composition and quantity of workers in Mexico changed—because they left. It's possible the immigrant used to make only $4 an hour at the teddy bear plant, and after they left, the factory had to offer a higher wage to find a replacement. Or it may be possible that the factory had to close altogether since replacing the emigrating workers was too expensive—so you won't even be able to find a teddy bear factory employee if you go back to Mexico. These types of issues seem incredibly hypothetical, but they are real enough to screw up your results if you took your proposed approach. Remember, we have nearly 10% of Mexico's population here in the United States, which is clearly enough of a change in Mexico's work force to affect the underlying labor market structure.

It is understood that the distribution of wages in the United States is different from the distribution of wages in Mexico. What is the source of this difference? Part of this is due to the fact that skills are different in the two countries—Mexico has an abundance of lower-skill labor, and it follows that they have an abundance of lower wages. The densities may look something like those in Figure 4.4.

However, not all of the distributional differences can be attributed to differences in skill level. It's possible that a worker with a certain level of skill, say s^*, gets paid $12 an hour in the United States and only $7 an hour in Mexico. This difference in wage is not due to differences in skill—the worker has skill level s^* in both countries. The wage difference is due to the fact that the price for skill is different in the two locations. Since we are interested in comparing the skill level of immigrants to that of natives, we need to figure out a way to isolate the effect of skills on wages from the effect of prices on wages.

Let $f_i(w|s)$ be the conditional distribution of wages in country i given skill level s. Define $D_i = 1$ if a worker is in the labor force in country i, and $D_i = 0$ otherwise. Let $h(s|i = mx, D_i = 1)$ be the distribution of skills in Mexico for all people in the labor force, and let $h(s|i = us, D_i = 1)$ be the distribution of skills in the United States for immigrant workers from Mexico who are in the labor force. (Functions lettered "h" are for Mexican workers.) The observed density of wages in Mexico is can be written as the following:

$$g(w \mid i = mx, D_i = 1) = \int f_{mx}(w \mid s) \cdot h(s \mid i = mx, D_i = 1)ds.$$

The interpretation of the function above is more straightforward than it may seem. What are the odds that a randomly selected worker in Mexico—someone in the labor force—makes exactly $w an hour? Well, the person I pick at random has a certain skill level, we have called it s. So what are the odds that a person with that particular skill—exactly s amount of skill—makes $w? Notice that not all people with skill level s will make $w an hour—some workers with skill s will make more than $w, some workers with skill s will make less than $w. The probability that, given the particular skill level s, you make $w an hour is given by the function $f_{mx}(w|s)$. Now, what are the changes that a randomly selected person has this particular level of skill? Some randomly selected workers will have more skill than s and some workers will have less skill than s—the probability that the one person I pick at random has a skill level of exactly s is given by $h(s|i = mx, D_i = 1)$. The odds that I pick a person with skill s multiplied by the odds that skill s makes $w is equal to the odds that I randomly pick a worker making $w. The integral is there to indicate that I have to pick workers at random over and over again until I have selected a worker with each possible level of skill. The result is the observed density of wages in Mexico. (I pick only workers—stay-at-home moms, students, and retired people are not in the group from which I'm selecting.)

Similarly, the observed density of wages in the United States, for immigrant workers from Mexico, is given by:

$$g(w \mid i = us, D_i = 1) = \int f_{us}(w \mid s) \cdot h(s \mid i = us, D_i = 1)ds.$$

Keep in mind, this gives us the odds that a randomly selected immigrant makes $w an hour. We have to select a worker who has immigrated from Mexico—we cannot select a native worker. (Functions with the letter h are for Mexican workers, regardless of where they are working.) So now we have the distribution of wages for Mexican workers both in Mexico and in the United States, as a function of skill level. From here, we will be able to back out the distribution of skills for these workers. We start with wages because wages can be observed. We have to figure out the distribution of skills because skills cannot be observed.

Notice that the probability that a randomly selected worker in Mexico has skill s will certainly be different from the probability that a randomly selected immigrant worker in the United States has skill s. This is due to the fact that immigrants immigrated for a reason and those who didn't immigrate stayed for a reason—i.e., these people are different. So, their skills will be different on average. This means that the functions $h(s|i = mx, D_i = 1)$ and $h(s|i = us, D_i = 1)$ will be different. There are a couple of explanations for this. First, there are differences in characteristics of these workers. One worker migrated, while the other did not—clear evidence that the two are different somehow. This will contribute to differences in observed skill levels in each location. Second, there will be differences in who satisfies $D_i = 1$. The skill level of those who choose to be in the labor force in Mexico will certainly differ from the skill level of those who choose to be in the labor force in the United States. Maybe only the highest-skilled workers choose to work in the United States since our welfare system works better than its Mexican counterpart, for example. Whatever the reason, it is logical that a person working in one location may not be working if they instead lived elsewhere, so $D_i = 1$ in location A for that person, but $D_i = 0$ in location B for the same person.

The next step is to construct a hypothetical distribution of wages for immigrants describing how much an immigrant currently working in the United States would make if they were paid according to Mexican prices. This will eventually eliminate the contribution of different prices in the distribution of wages. Notice that this distribution is not observed—immigrants working in the United States are paid according to United States standards, not Mexican standards—so it is impossible for us to observe these wages. This theoretical or hypothetical distribution is written as follows:

$$\tilde{g}(w) = \int f_{mx}(w \mid s) \cdot h(s \mid i = us, D_i = 1) ds.$$

This looks similar to the g(·) functions from earlier, but the arguments of the integral are different. The function $f_{mx}(w|s)$ is the distribution of wages (conditioned on skill) in Mexico—this is the probability that a worker with skill level s gets \$w an hour in Mexico. The function $h(s|i = us, D_i = 1)$ is the distribution of skill in the United States—this is the odds that a randomly chosen immigrant worker in the United States has skill level s. So we pick a worker randomly in the United States, determine their skill level, and then see what a worker with that exact skill level would likely be paid in Mexico.

Rewrite the integral above as follows:

$$\int f_{mx}(w \mid s) \cdot h(s \mid i = us, D_i = 1) ds = \int f_{mx}(w \mid s) \cdot h(s \mid i = us, D_i = 1) \cdot \frac{h(s \mid i = mx, D_i = 1)}{h(s \mid i = mx, D_i = 1)} ds.$$

Since this is merely multiplication by one on the right-hand side, nothing has changed. To simplify, let's write

$$= \int \theta f_{mx}(w \mid s) \cdot h(s \mid i = mx, D_i = 1) ds$$

where

$$\theta = \frac{h(s \mid i = us, D_i = 1)}{h(s \mid i = mx, D_i = 1)}.$$

Recall Bayes' Law:

$$\Pr(A \mid B) = \Pr(B \mid A) \cdot \frac{\Pr(A)}{\Pr(B)}.$$

We will use Bayes' Law to rewrite

$$\Pr(i = us, D_i = 1 \mid s) = h(s \mid i = us, D_i = 1) \cdot \frac{\Pr(i = us, D_i = 1)}{h(s)}$$

where we have used the following substitutions for A and B: $i = us, D_i = 1$ is A, s is B. Don't forget that $h(\cdot)$ is the same as $\Pr(\cdot)$, so this fits into the formula for Bayes' Law nicely. Rearrange again to get

$$h(s) = \frac{h(s \mid i = us, D_i = 1) \cdot \Pr(i = us, D_i = 1)}{\Pr(i = us, D_i = 1 \mid s)}.$$

A similar rearrangement for the case of $i = mx$ will give us

$$h(s) = \frac{h(s \mid i = mx, D_i = 1) \cdot \Pr(i = mx, D_i = 1)}{\Pr(i = mx, D_i = 1 \mid s)}.$$

We now have two expressions for $h(s)$, so we can set them equal to each other:

$$\frac{h(s \mid i = us, D_i = 1) \cdot \Pr(i = us, D_i = 1)}{\Pr(i = us, D_i = 1 \mid s)} = h(s) = \frac{h(s \mid i = mx, D_i = 1) \cdot \Pr(i = mx, D_i = 1)}{\Pr(i = mx, D_i = 1 \mid s)}.$$

If we group terms so that everything with an h is on the left side, we get

$$\frac{h(s \mid i = us, D_i = 1)}{h(s \mid i = mx, D_i = 1)} = \frac{\Pr(i = mx, D_i = 1) \cdot \Pr(i = us, D_i = 1 \mid s)}{\Pr(i = us, D_i = 1) \cdot \Pr(i = mx, D_i = 1 \mid s)}.$$

The fraction on the left is θ, just as we defined it earlier. The numerator of the fraction on the left is unknown since it cannot be observed (it is the hypothetical distribution of wages for immigrants if they were paid in Mexico). Determining this was our main obstacle. However, everything on the right side of the equal sign is known—it is the probability that a Mexican worker works in the United States and the probability that a Mexican worker works in Mexico. So, if we want to undertake the enormous task of collected data on workers in both the United States and Mexico,

Figure 4.5

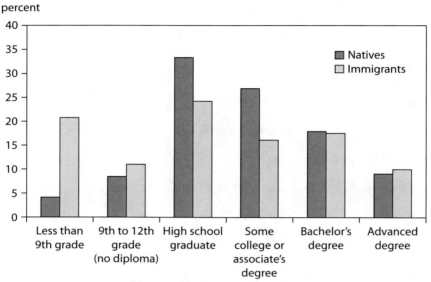

Educational attainment of immigrants and natives, March 2003

Note: Data are for immigrants and natives 25 and older.
Source: March 2003 Current Population Survey.

Table 4.5[10]

The Changing Skills of the Immigrant and Native Populations, 1960–98

	1960	1970	1980	1990	1998
Native men					
Percent who are high school dropouts	53.0	39.7	23.3	11.9	9.0
Percent who are college graduates	11.4	15.4	22.8	26.4	29.8
Percent with at least a master's degree	—	—	—	9.2	9.9
Immigrant men					
Percent who are high school dropouts	66.0	49.0	37.5	31.4	33.6
Percent who are college graduates	10.1	18.6	25.3	26.6	28.3
Percent with at least a master's degree	—	—	—	12.9	12.5
Percent hourly wage differential between immigrant and native men	4.2	0.0	−9.2	−15.0	−23.0
Native women					
Percent who are high school dropouts	46.1	35.3	19.7	9.2	6.6
Percent who are college graduates	9.7	11.5	17.9	23.6	28.5
Percent with at least a master's degree	—	—	—	7.7	8.7
Immigrant women					
Percent who are high school dropouts	61.8	47.9	34.6	25.9	24.5
Percent who are college graduates	5.6	9.7	17.5	23.0	28.7
Percent with at least a master's degree	—	—	—	8.0	8.8
Percent hourly wage differential between immigrant and native women	3.4	3.0	−1.7	−5.0	−12.1

---

[10] Borjas, *Heaven's Door*, p. 21.

we can use this formula to estimate the skill difference between immigrant worker and those who stayed in Mexico. Some statistics are in the following section.

Evidence of Skills of Immigrants

Unfortunately, skill is not something that can be easily observed. However, there are a couple of very good proxies for skill: education or even wage (assuming the market works efficiently). How do immigrants compare to natives in these categories for the United States? Does the empirical evidence support the theories outlined previously? On page 84, Figure 4.5 gives a starting point to answer these questions.[11]

I hope that the first thing you notice is that Figure 4.5 is merely a snapshot taken during 2003. It does not capture how education or skill of immigrants and natives has evolved over time. That said, what does the figure tell us so far? It looks like the propensity of immigrants to have low education levels is much greater than for natives. Interestingly, although more immigrants than natives never attend high school, the same can be said about advanced degrees. So immigrants are either really smart or completely uneducated—at least that seems to be the case in 2003. Does this conclusion change if we consider other periods? Has immigration policy impacted the relative education level of immigrants to natives? Table 4.5 takes a look in this direction.

An important policy change to remember when interpreting Table 4.5 is that which took place in the mid-1960s, when the United States shifted priority of its immigration policy from job skills to family reunification. As you can see, there are both differences and similarities in relative education level between immigrants and natives over time. Both groups (and both genders) have reduced the number of high school dropouts considerably over this period of time (although in percentage terms the native reduction is greater). Likewise, both groups have increased the percentage of their population who are college graduates (although the natives again outpace immigrants in percentage terms). However, despite these similarities, the wage differential has gone from favoring immigrants to greatly favoring native workers.

Based on these data alone, it may appear that the skill level of immigrants has shifted from skilled (well, from less unskilled) to unskilled. What other explanation could there be for the fact that the education rate and wages of natives seems to have outpaced that of immigrants? Have immigrants been underperforming natives in terms of educational attainment? The following figure supports the idea that, taken as a whole, the trend for immigrants to be less educated has not driven down the overall education level of immigrant states.

In Figure 4.6, the line labeled "other immigrant states" refers to the five most popular locations for immigrants to settle (we'll discuss this at length in a bit). For

---

[11] Hanson, "Why Does Immigration Divide America", p. 20.

now, just know that California is number one in immigrant population, and most of the rest of immigrants live in only a handful of "immigrant states." As it appears, these popular immigrant locations seem to be getting relatively smarter than the rest of the country. That is to say that the ratio of college graduates per high school dropout has increased more for immigrant locations. (Obviously there are immigrants in the non-"immigrant states" too.) Is this consistent with the data from Table 4.5? It seems to be contrary. The table implies immigrants have become relatively less skilled, while the figure implies immigrants have outpaced natives. How do we explain this? There are a couple of plausible explanations. We know that immigrants are abundant in California. (This argument will hold for any of the immigrant states.) We also know that immigrants tend to be less educated than natives, as we saw in Table 4.5. So why does it appear that areas with high concentration of less-educated immigrants are getting smarter? What if highly educated natives are drawn to areas where less-educated immigrants are common? This would result in the trends shown in Figure 4.6. (We'll discuss why this would be the case later.) Alternately, it might be possible that highly educated natives are drawn to California for reasons independent of immigrants. Maybe it's the sunshine. (However, in order for this to be true, we would have to justify why educated people would be more attracted to sunshine than their uneducated counterparts. I would think the sunshine would attract both educated and uneducated equally. Actually, uneducated workers who have to work outside might be

Figure 4.6[12]

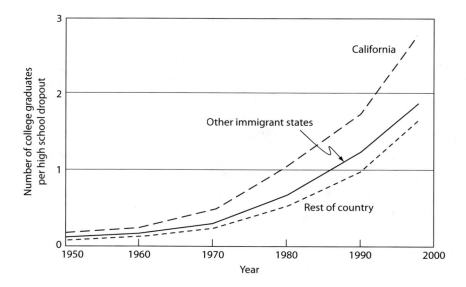

12 Figure taken from Borjas, *Heaven's Door*, p. 79.

more attracted to sunshine than their educated counterparts.) It is also possible that uneducated immigrants arrive and then become educated. Maybe they all come here to go to school. (The explanations are getting weaker now.) Whatever the explanation, it is important that you realize that the fact that there is no obvious answer to these questions is actually one of the reasons the immigration debate is still ongoing. It's hard to complain about uneducated immigrants in California if California is getting smarter as a result of immigration. One thing we can say for sure is this: lately, it appears that immigrants are less educated than natives, but we could use more evidence about how this affects us.

Wages of Immigrants

Table 4.5 showed that immigrants make less per hour than natives (23% less for men, 12% less for women). This is consistent with the finding that immigrants tend to be less educated than natives in recent periods. Do we see similar trends for annual wages among immigrants versus natives? Do immigrants make less than natives in a given year (which would be logical) or is the hourly wage difference mitigated by longer hours? Figure 4.7 gives an overview of recent data.

Technically you can't tell who makes more money from this figure, since "$75,000 and above" could include ridiculously high wages belonging to the few immigrants

Figure 4.7[13]

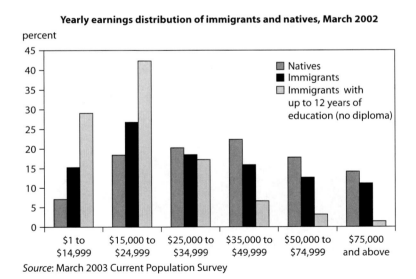

Source: March 2003 Current Population Survey

---

[13] Hanson, "Why Does Immigration Divide America?" p. 22.

in that group. However, the trend is clear: natives' average income is higher than immigrants'. Notice the big difference between immigrants with fewer than 12 years of education and the rest of the immigrant population. It's likely this group is driving some of the trends we have seen in previous sections.

So we have two reliable conclusions at this point; one concerning the lower education rate of immigrants and a second concerning the lower earnings of immigrants. Keep in mind, both of these observations are true today, but historically they did not hold. In fact, as Table 4.5 showed, immigrants used to earn a higher average wage than natives. The change over time of relative earnings and education may be the result of policy decisions concerning immigration (recall the major policy changes in 1965). Table 4.6 breaks down wage data by region of origin, which highlights some of the changes since 1965.

Notice the shift from European and Canadian immigrants to Mexican, Latin American, and Asian countries of origin. Some of this can be attributed to policy changes during this period. Also notice the wage differential for each group. Taken together, these data may help explain why we have seen a reduction in relative wages for immigrants as compared to natives. It seems plausible that a randomly selected immigrant from any particular region is just as skilled today as they were 30 years ago, but the composition of regions represented has changed over time.

To further confuse the issue, consider Figure 4.8, which shows wage differential based on when an immigrant arrives in the United States.

Table 4.6[14]

	Link between National Origin and the Decline in the Relative Wage of Immigrants		
	Percent of immigrants born in region		Percent wage differential between immigrant and native men
	1970	1990	
Region of birth			
Asia	10.8	25.3	−4.4
Europe and Canada	60.8	20.5	18.1
Mexico	10.0	24.9	−40.1
Other Latin America	13.8	22.2	−22.4
Other	4.6	7.1	−16.4
Actual wage gap in 1970			0.0
Actual wage gap in 1990			−15.8
Predicate wage gap in 1990 if the immigrants had the 1970 national origin mix			0.2

---

[14] Borjas, *Heaven's Door*, p. 44.

At first glance, this figure seems straight-forward and condemning of recent immigrant skill. As time passes, immigrant wages continually fall compared to native wages. The immediate conclusion is that since immigrant wages are worsening, so must their skill level. Thus, *waves of immigrants are becoming less skilled over time.* This is a major issue in light of the fact that these changes seem to coincide with the change in United States immigration policy that lessened the importance of job skills and increased the importance of family reunification. If this policy change results in each wave of immigrants being less capable than the prior wave, then this policy should perhaps be questioned. However, this conclusion may be hastily made.

A second interpretation of this same diagram is this: all immigrants have the same skill upon arrival, and they increase their skill level (and thus their wage) over time as they assimilate to life in the United States. As time goes by, the immigrants who arrived between 1985 and 1989 (who currently make over 30% less than natives) will improve their skill and earnings so that in 35 to 40 years, they will be making almost 30% more than natives. This conclusion is just as valid as the prior one, and it is completely contrary in the sense that it does not bring to question the change in United States immigration policy with the same severity. The complaint still could be made however, that it is intolerable to allow uneducated immigrants to arrive—even if they do empirically become high-skilled over time. However, if the assimilation explanation holds, I think even people making an argument against immigration would have to agree that the situation could be worse.

Unfortunately, in light of other evidence we have seen, it's probably safe to assume

Figure 4.8[15]

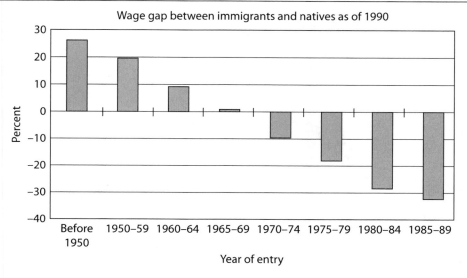

Wage gap between immigrants and natives as of 1990

Year of entry

---

[15] Figure taken from Borjas, *Heaven's Door*, p. 24.

that the former conclusion is correct—that each subsequent wave of immigrants is less skilled than the previous. Not only are they less skilled than natives (who are becoming more skilled over time), but they appear to be less skilled than earlier generations of immigrants.

So what do we take from this evidence? It is clear that today, on average, immigrants make less than natives. Education levels are lower for immigrants, and (as we will see) the types of occupations are different. However, many of these recent findings are just that—recent. The tendency of an average immigrant to make less and to know less has appeared only during the past couple of decades. This is likely a symptom of policy. For example, we know that the most popular region from which immigrants arrive has shifted from Europe to Latin America thanks to changes in policy. A comparison of education level by region is more revealing than comparing education level over time—it's the change in the mix of country of origin that is primarily driving these results. Immigrants from Germany are just as skilled today as they were 50 years ago. Likewise, immigrants from Mexico are just as skilled as they were 50 years ago. The difference is that there are many more immigrants from Mexico (and fewer from Germany) relative to 50 years ago, which causes the average skill level to change.

Despite these findings, we still see some confusing data occasionally. For example, the data behind Figure 4.6 and some of the predictions of the Roy Models are difficult to interpret. Overall, I think we can conclude the following with great confidence: the issue of skill of immigrants is not a simple matter.

Chapter 5

Immigrants and Labor Markets

Do We Need Immigrant Workers?

Why does our current immigration policy allow people to enter the country, at least in part, based on job skills? Why do we allow immigration at all, for that matter? We do have the technology and ability to prevent nearly all immigration, both legal and illegal. True, some people would slip through the cracks, regardless of how strict our policy may become, but we really don't make much of an effort in the United States currently. There are not random checks, no tracking of people, almost anybody can get a driver's license—or go to school. Certainly anybody can walk around freely without being harassed into proving their immigration status. Why? The reason is that we must perceive some measurable benefit of having immigrants enter the United States, including for work-related reasons. Since "job skills" is one of the four pillars of our immigration policy, we must conclude this: immigrant workers are good for our economy. But why exactly is this true?

Your first instinct might be to say something along the lines of "immigrants take jobs that nobody else wants." Although this could possibly be true (we'll look for evidence in a minute), would this fact really justify importing workers? Think of a job that fits the description you gave that "nobody else wants" it. Why doesn't anybody else want it? Probably because the wage rate for that particular job is too low. If so, it would be more accurate to say "immigrants take jobs that nobody else wants…at the current wage rate." But now you've said something different because there are now two ways to solve this problem—immigration is one, or we could instead simply adjust the wage rate so that some native workers change their mind about not wanting that job. Why is immigration the better option?

Essentially the argument outlined in the previous paragraph deals with using immigration to address labor shortage issues. This is a particularly popular topic in places like Japan, where the labor force is rapidly aging and replacements seem to be hard to find. (We will revisit this in a later chapter.) However, the idea of "labor shortage" is a tricky thing to think about. When do we typically see shortages? As the figure below shows, a shortage is the result of a price (or wage) that is below equilibrium.

Figure 5.1

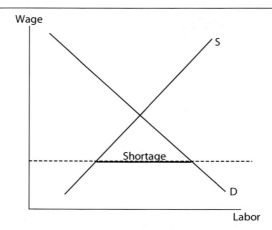

What this implies for a labor market is not that we don't have enough people to do all the work we want to have done—it simply means that, *at the current wage*, not enough people are willing to enter the labor force. The people are there, they just don't want to work for such a low wage. This hidden reserve of workers can be used—and immigrant labor can be foregone—as long as we can drive wages up sufficiently to induce entry into the labor market.

Now, as is typically the case, nothing is without cost. What are the costs of this suggestion above? As wages rise, so do prices. Thus, eliminating our reliance on immigrant labor may result in higher prices. This is, in fact, a result that we will see often in the material that follows—immigrants tend to make things cheaper. Not because they are willing to do jobs that nobody else wants, but because they are willing to do jobs for less money than are natives.

So, to answer the question posed in the section heading: do we need immigrant workers? The answer is "no." However, these workers may be the welfare-maximizing (think CS + PS kind of welfare!) factor for our economy—they may make the economic pie bigger.

Do Immigrants Take Jobs Nobody Else Wants?

You may have speculated that the fact that immigrants take jobs that natives refuse is behind some of the results we saw in the previous section. It may be possible that immigrant workers are just as skilled as natives, but (for reasons unrelated to skill) they take undesirable jobs, which drives down their wage. To explore this possibility, it seems logical to dig up data on immigrant versus native workers by industry. If it is in fact the case that immigrants are taking primarily low-skilled jobs (and thus driving down immigrant average wage), then we should see a noticeable difference in the distribution of immigrant workers by sector. Let's start with Figure 5.2.

Figure 5.2[1]

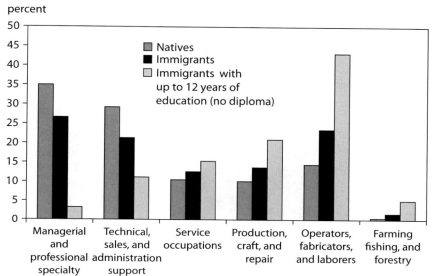

Occupational distribution of immigrants and natives, March 2003

Source: March 2003 Current Population Survey.

Two striking things hopefully pop out at you from Figure 5.2. The first is that there is a big difference between an average immigrant and the group of the most-uneducated immigrants. This can be seen in the "Operators, fabricators, and laborers" category, which is not very popular among natives or the average immigrant, but seems to be very popular for uneducated immigrants. (If we had separated natives into educated and uneducated, we may see a similar trend for natives as well.) The second is that there is in fact a difference between natives and immigrants (although not a very big one). More natives seem to be working in managerial positions and technical fields while immigrants dominate service, production, and farming areas. However, please notice that the difference is never greater than 10%. Table 5.1 provides some more specific numbers:

---

[1] Hanson, "Why Does Immigration Divide America?" p. 21.

Table 5.1²

Occupations and Industries Employing Immigrants and Natives, 1995

	Percent of immigrants employed in occupation or industry	Percent of natives employed in occupation or industry	Percent of workers in occupation or industry who are foreign-born
Occupations			
Managerial and professional specialty	21.2	28.2	7.6
Technical and related support	2.5	3.2	7.7
Sales	9.4	12.1	7.9
Administrative support, including clerical	9.7	15.4	6.4
Precision, production, craft, and repair	11.7	11.0	10.5
Operators and fabricators	14.9	10.5	13.5
Handlers, equipment cleaners, helpers, and laborers	5.7	4.2	12.9
Private household	2.1	0.5	31.5
Service (excluding private household)	17.4	12.5	13.3
Farming, forestry, and fishing	5.4	2.5	19.4
Industry			
Agriculture	5.0	2.3	19.0
Mining	0.3	0.6	5.1
Construction	6.4	6.6	9.7
Manufacturing	20.2	16.2	12.0
Transport, communication, and utilities	5.3	7.2	7.5
Wholesale trade	4.4	3.9	11.0
Retail trade	17.7	16.5	10.5
Finance, insurance, real estate	5.0	6.3	7.9
Services	33.4	35.1	9.5
Government	2.3	5.2	4.5

The first and second columns provide the proportion of immigrant and native populations that are employed in each industry. The last column gives the percentage of total workers in each industry who are not native. For example, only 5% of the immigrant population is employed in agriculture, but that 5% represents nearly 20% of the total agricultural workers.

At first glance, there doesn't seem to be that many striking differences between natives and immigrants. However, pay special attention to "Operators and fabricators," "Service," "Farming, forestry, and fishing," and "Agriculture." In percentage terms, far more immigrants are employed in these sectors. The opposite is true about "Administrative support" and "Government." Keep in mind, the difference between

---

² Borjas, "Heaven's Door", p. 80.

2.3% and 5.2% may not seem significant (it's a difference of less than 3% after all), but in percentage terms, that is more than double the amount of native workers.

Although it seems like we're working our way toward a possible explanation for the wage gap between immigrants and natives based on quality of jobs performed by each, don't get swept away thinking that immigrants are likely to take crappy and dangerous jobs. For example, on average, natives are employed in positions that experience 4.6 injuries annually per 100 workers, compared to 4.4 injuries per 100 for immigrants. Also, about 8% of natives work the midnight shift—exactly the same as their immigrant counterparts. So it seems that immigrants and natives are equally prone to take undesirable jobs.

It is undeniable that there are some differences between the average immigrant occupation and that of their native counterparts. However, are immigrants merely responding to market forces, or is the immigrant population so large that it actually drives these results? Are immigrants simply taking jobs in low-paying sectors, or has the abundance of immigrants in certain areas in the United States actually driven down wages?

How Do Immigrants Affect Labor Markets?

How immigration affects labor markets is one of the biggest topics at the center of the immigration debate. Do they steal our jobs? Do immigrants drive down wages? Does immigration increase the amount of unemployment? All of these questions are easily explored using the simple tools we have already covered. (If you answer "yes" to "do immigrants drive down wages?" then you probably shouldn't say "yes" to "does immigration increase the amount of unemployment?" If the wage rate adjusts to compensate for immigration, then there should be no excess supply of workers as a result. This can be shown via a simple supply/demand diagram. True, it is possible for the wage to adjust, but not completely, resulting in both a lower wage and more unemployment, but please recognize that wage adjustment mitigates the unemployment issue.)

No matter how immigration affects us, there is one important thing to recognize: immigration must affect labor markets in the short run. Please don't ignore the last part of that sentence: "in the short run." The reason the short run is an important detail is that certain things in the economy are assumed to be fixed in the short run. For example, the number of jobs, or the number of firms in a particular area may be constant in the short run, but flexible in the long run. The difference, as we will see, can be profound.

Figure 5.3

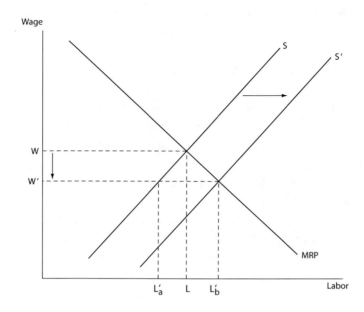

Theory of How Immigrants Affect Labor Markets

Partial Equilibrium Analysis

Everything that follows assumes a competitive labor market. Non-competitive markets are beyond the scope of this text. In addition, special care will be taken to differentiate the SR effects from the LR effects. When we analyze labor markets, we have to take care to specify the particular industry, sector, or region we are considering. For example, "metal worker" is different from "steel worker," which is different from "sheet metal worker," and this is different from "sheet metal worker in California," and so on. I'll present everything generically, but please realize that results will vary as your definition of markets or regions changes.

If immigrant labor and native labor are substitutes for each other, then immigration increases the number of workers in the labor force, which is illustrated by a rightward shift of the labor-supply curve. As a result of this shift, the prevailing wage rate will fall. This is a short-run effect, and is pictured in Figure 5.3.

Notice that before immigration, L people we employed in this market, all of them native. After immigration, the number of people working increases to L'_b, but the number of natives employed falls to L'_a ($L'_b - L'_a$ is the amount of immigrant workers). So the short-run effect of immigration is more total workers in this market, but fewer natives than before.

Figure 5.4

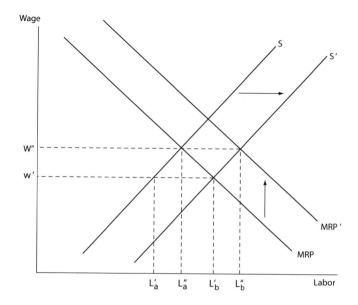

What changes in the long run? Firms see that wages in this particular region have fallen, and as result of the now-cheaper labor resource, the region becomes more at-tractive to anybody who hires labor. This creates an increase in capital investment in the region, and as the amount of capital increases, so will productivity of labor. As we know, when labor becomes more productive, the MRP curve shifts up. As a result, wage will also be driven up—how far up depends on the size of the shift. Thus, in the long run, wages may end up being lower, higher, or the same as they were prior to the increase in labor due to immigration. Figure 5.4 shows the coincidental case where the shift in the MRP curve exactly offsets the initial change in supply—this is not always the case!

Notice that, in the LR, the number of total workers increases from L'_b to L''_b. Further, the number of natives employed in this market increases from L'_a to L''_a, which in this particular case is exactly equal to the original number employed before immigration (L). Please recognize that if the demand shifted less than what is pictured, the number of natives working in the LR would be less than L, and if the demand shift was greater than pictured, more than L natives would be working. Also please recognize that the supply and demand curves are drawn parallel here—a detail that may not be true in reality. Thus, the number of immigrants employed in the LR ($L''_b - L''_a$) may be different from the number employed in the SR ($L'_b - L'_a$).

How about the case when immigrant labor and native labor are complements? If immigrants have different skills from natives, then an increase in immigration will free

Figure 5.5

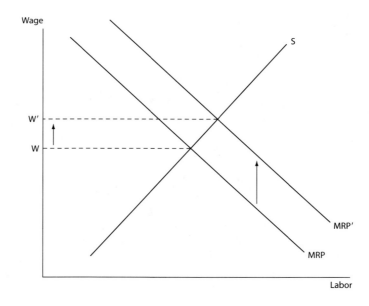

up native labor and allow natives to specialize. This will increase productivity of labor, and shift the MRP curve upward in the SR (see Figure 5.5).

What is the LR change in this case? Well, potential workers (both native and immigrant) in the area who are currently not in the labor force (like students and retired people) will see the higher wages and decide to enter the labor force. Additionally, workers from other areas will see that wages in this region have increased, and they may decide to relocate to take advantage. Either way, the supply of labor should increase in the LR and the wage rate will be driven back down (not necessarily to the original *w*).

We have shown that we expect wages to adjust to immigration in the SR if labor markets are competitive, and this effect should disappear somewhat (or completely) in the LR. You may want to argue the assumption that labor markets are competitive—they are probably not. For example, immigrants can't legally work in the United States unless they are LPRs or have some other agreement or permissible visa. This prevents entry into the labor market. Things like unions and monopsonies are also considerations. In essence, our assumption that labor markets are competitive may result in inconsistent empirical evidence.

All of these effects should be measurable both in the destination country and in the country of origin. A rightward shift of the supply curve here must be mirrored with a leftward shift there, since they are experiencing a loss of workers. This in turn will drive up wages there in the SR, and the demand curve will shift down in the LR to mitigate the SR effect. We will revisit this later when we discuss the welfare implications of immigration.

General Equilibrium Analysis

In the previous section, we examined how a movement of labor from one region to another affects either the supply or demand for labor in both the destination and origin. For example, if low-skill workers move from Mexico to the United States, the supply curve for low-skill labor will shift to the right in the United States and to the left in Mexico. This is called partial equilibrium because it focuses on only one market at a time—either low skill *or* high skill, not both. What we will do here considers the effect of labor movements on both high- and low-skill industries simultaneously in both the United States and Mexico. We call this general equilibrium (GE).[3]

We start by developing a graphical representation of the kinds of labor firms in each country want to hire. So think about a random firm, let's say it produces toasters. Toasters require both high- and low-skill labor to manufacture. Some high-skill labor includes the engineers who adjust the machinery, computer programmers, and toast experts, while low-skill labor includes people to package the toasters and sweep the floors. How much of each type of labor should the firm hire? The answer depends on a couple of things, like how much each kind of labor costs, how productive each kind of labor is, and how many toasters they want to produce.

So let's say they want to produce 1,000 toasters each day. This firm wants to know all combinations of high-skill and low-skill labor that will result in this level of output. Obviously, if they cut back on one low-skill worker, the plant output slows down a

Figure 5.6

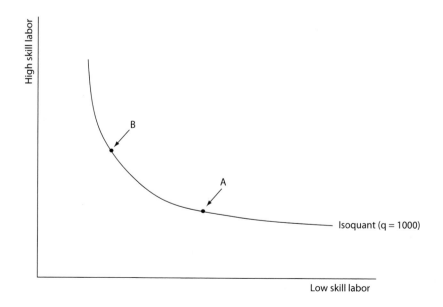

Figure 5.7

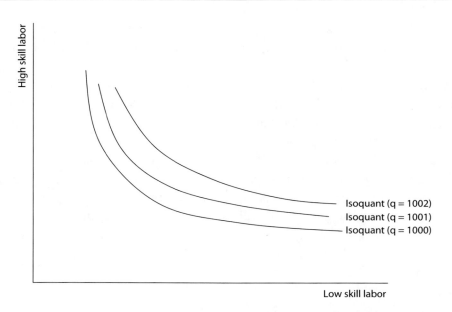

little, so they would need to add a fraction of a high-skilled worker to compensate (yes, you can have fractions of people). We can conclude that there are at least two different combinations of workers that will yield 1,000 toasters—lots of low-skill and few high-skill (point A) and lots of high-skill and few low-skill (point B). If we continued to find other combinations of high- and low-skilled workers that resulted in 1,000 toasters and graphed all of these points, it would look something like the diagram in Figure 5.6.

We call this line an "isoquant" since all points on this curve will produce exactly 1,000 toasters. You can think of this as a firm's indifference curve—where the firm is indifferent between point A and point B since both produce 1,000 toasters. The firm will have hundreds and thousands of these isoquants, one corresponding to every possible level of output. Further away from the origin, output would go up, as the figure below indicates.

Isoquants can never intersect. If they did then there would be one combination of workers that would result in two different levels of output (one for each isoquant that touches the point of intersection).

All of this is great, but we still need to answer one important question—how much low-skill and high-skill labor should the firm hire? We don't have all the information we need to answer this just yet. We have graphed a relationship between workers and output, but we have yet to consider how much these workers cost. Obviously, if point

Figure 5.8

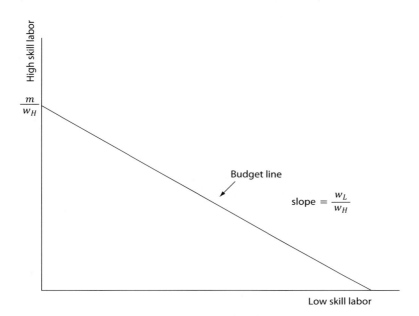

A produces the same number of toasters as point B, then the firm will pick the cheaper of the two. Why pay more for point B when point A gives you the same output for less cost?

Assume low-skill labor cost $\$w_L$ (w is for wage) and high-skill labor cost $\$w_H$. Further assume that the firm has $\$m$ available to spend on labor (m stands for money). Drop the dollar signs, and it follows that $m = w_L \cdot L + w_H \cdot H$.

Rearrange this by moving the low-skilled terms to the left side of the equal sign,

$$m - w_L \cdot L = w_H \cdot H$$

and then divide both sides by w_H

$$\frac{m}{w_H} - \frac{w}{w_H} \cdot L = H$$

which is merely the equation for a line with a y-intercept of $\frac{m}{w_H}$ and a slope of $\frac{w_L}{w_H}$. We know how to graph lines, as shown below. (This line is called the *budget line*.)[4]

---

[4] Technically, it's an isocost curve.

Figure 5.9

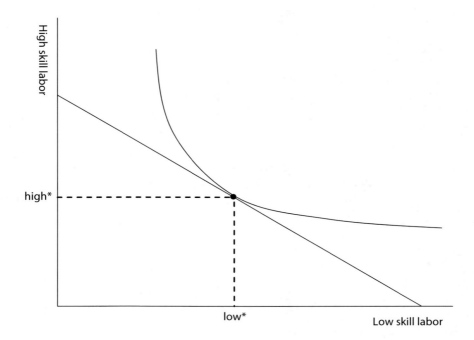

Now that we have a graphical representation of who the firm wants to hire and who the firm can afford to hire, we can combine these to get a picture of who the firm will hire (see Figure 5.9).

Notice that the position of the budget line is fixed—it is determined by things like wages (which are not determined by the firm). So, faced with these prices, the firm will try to produce as many toasters as possible without overspending their budget. The firm arrives at the optimal point (low*, high*) by moving up isoquants until they just barely touch the budget line.

So far so good, but we have only looked at one firm, and you've been promised that this general equilibrium will work for multiple firms (in Mexico and the United States) simultaneously. To extend what we have here to apply to more than one production location, we need to complicate the story a little.

Let's talk about the United States and Mexico. If we add up all of the labor in both countries, we would get the total amount of low-skilled and high-skilled labor that is available to work in either country. This is the *initial endowment* of labor. Some of the low-skilled labor belongs to the United States (the United States' share of the initial endowment), and some of the low-skilled labor belongs to Mexico (Mexico's share of the initial endowment). The same is true for high-skilled labor. Notice also that if the United States uses one low-skilled worker, then that worker is no longer available for

Figure 5.10

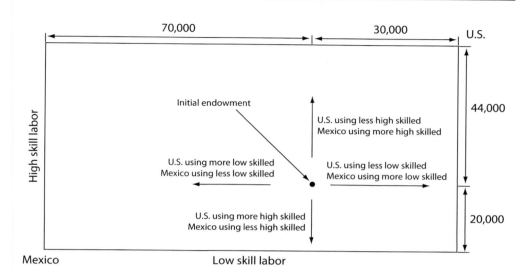

Mexico to use. The more low-skilled labor used by the United States, the less available for Mexico. Again, the same holds for high-skilled labor.

The way we will show this give and take between the two countries is to draw a box, labeling the lower-left corner "Mexico" and the upper-right corner "United States." That is to say that the lower-left corner of the box is Mexico's origin (zero low-skilled, zero high-skilled)—and this point is very far from the upper-right corner of the box, which is the United States' origin. If the United States is at a point very far from their origin, then they are using lots of low-skilled and lots of high-skilled labor—a fact consistent with Mexico's using zero of both. Thus, if we start at the initial endowment (which is represented by a dot in the box) and move left, Mexico is using less low-skilled labor, while the United States is using more. Vertical movements represent changes in high-skilled labor, as illustrated in Figure 5.10.

The size of the box above is determined by how much low-skilled labor exists, while the height of the box represents how much high-skilled labor exists. For example, if there are 100,000 low-skilled and 64,000 high-skilled workers, then the box would be 100,000 units wide and 64,000 units tall, as shown. Of the 100,000 low-skilled workers, say 70,000 are Mexican along with 20,000 of the high-skilled labor. In this case, the endowment point would be positioned at (70,000, 20,000) from Mexico's origin—70,000 units to the right and 20,000 units above Mexico's origin. (Verify that this position is exactly 30,000 to the left and 44,000 below the origin for the United States). This box is called an *Edgeworth Box*.

The rest of the story follows similarly to the case of only one firm. Each country (or a random firm in each country) has indifference curves or isoquants (but the United

Figure 5.11

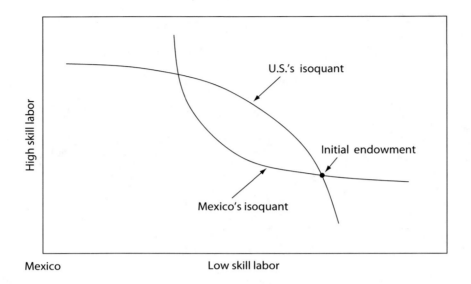

States' isoquants go the other way—down and left—since their origin is upside down), as shown in Figure 5.11.

The initial endowment is labeled, and I have drawn the particular isoquant that goes through the endowment point. Notice that the United States would be unhappy with any movement of labor that would result in their moving to a lower isoquant (since this migration would result in lower United States output), but they would welcome any movement of labor that would move them to a higher isoquant (since this migration results in increased United States output).

Just like before, we are going to be faced with a budget line. In fact, we will assume that firms in both countries are behaving in such a way that they are performing as well as possible given the budget they face (i.e., they are maximizing profit). This means that each country will have already chosen the highest isoquant possible given their budget constraint, so that their isoquant will be tangent to the budget line, as we saw in an earlier diagram.

Here's an important detail: wages in the United States are not the same as they are in Mexico. In fact, the ratio of high-skilled wage to low-skilled wage is different in the two countries. For example, Mexico has an abundance of low-skilled workers, so low-skilled labor will be cheap (small w_L) and high-skilled will be expensive (large w_H), resulting in a flat budget line (remember the slope of the budget line is $\frac{w_L}{w_H}$ as we showed above). In the United States, however, high-skilled labor is relatively more abundant and low-skilled labor is relatively more scarce, resulting in a different ratio of prices and a steeper budget line. It is important that you carefully read the word "relatively" in the previous sentence. When I say "low-skill labor is relatively more

Figure 5.12

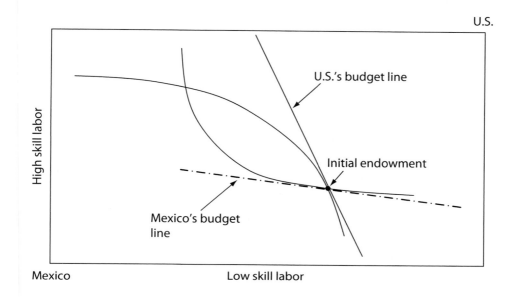

scarce" I am not saying that the United States has less low-skilled labor than Mexico. (They might—but they might not.) What I am saying is that there are fewer low-skilled workers per high-skilled worker so that the ratio is different.[5]

So, the United States should have a steeper budget line than Mexico, since the proportion of high-skilled to low-skilled labor is different in the two locations. Specifically, the slope of the budget line in the United States is $\frac{w_L^{US}}{w_H^{US}}$ while the slope of Mexico's budget line is $\frac{w_L^{mex}}{w_H^{mex}}$. Also, each country's isoquant should be tangent to their budget line at the endowment. This is illustrated in Figure 5.12.

How does labor migration affect this picture? Well, we know that $w_L^{mex} < w_L^{US}$ from the slopes of the budget lines above. As a result, low-skilled labor in Mexico wants to move to the United States to take advantage of the higher low-skilled wage there. This is reflected in the diagram by moving from the initial endowment to a point left of the initial endowment. (Recall that moving directly left is the case of Mexico using less low-skilled labor and the United States using more.) Once the allocation of labor moves, then the isoquants have to also move (they have to touch the allocation point). So the United States will move up to a higher isoquant and Mexico will move down to a lower isoquant. This makes sense given the fact that the United States is gaining labor (and thus gaining output) and Mexico is losing labor (and thus losing output). If the isoquants move, then the budget lines also must move—but they will not move parallel! If you start at a point on Mexico's isoquant and move to the left, tracing the isoquant as you go, what happens to the slope of the isoquant? It gets steeper. Since

---

[5] And it should probably be "scarcer" instead of "more scarce."

Figure 5.13

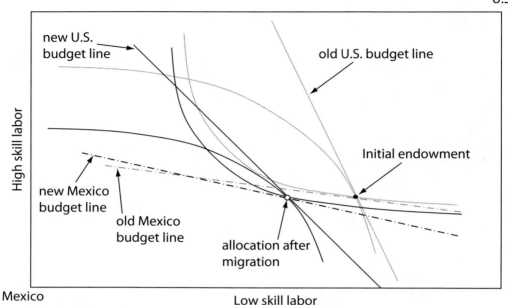

the migration from Mexico to the United States in this example moves the allocation to the left, Mexico's isoquant will be steeper at the new allocation than it was at the initial endowment. So too must the budget line be steeper since it will be tangent to the new isoquant. A similar argument will show that the United States' budget line will be flatter at the new allocation than it was at the initial endowment.

I have drawn all of this in Figure 5.13. There is a lot going on in this diagram, so take some time to process it. All of the original isoquants and budget lines from the diagram above are reproduced lightly in gray so that you can see how things have changed. Start by noticing the left movement from the endowment point.

Here is the point of all of this: migration must affect the relative prices for labor. Further, it must affect prices in both locations. This is clear from the slopes of each country's budget lines above. So, when we are looking for the effect of immigration on wages, that effect must be present—even if it's hiding.

Table 5.2[6]

Concentration of immigrants in six gateway US states						
	State share of total US population		State share of total US foreign-born population		Foreign-born share of total population	
State	**1994**	**2003**	**1994**	**2003**	**1994**	**2003**
California	12.3	12.3	34.0	27.5	22.5	27.8
New York	7.0	6.7	11.7	11.7	13.6	21.0
Florida	5.4	5.7	9.3	8.8	13.9	18.6
Texas	7.0	7.5	9.0	10.4	10.4	16.8
New Jersey	3.1	3.0	4.5	4.4	12.0	17.6
Illinois	4.5	4.4	4.7	4.4	8.6	12.1
United States	—	—	—	—	8.2	12.1

Source: March 1994 and 2003 Current Population Surveys.

Evidence of Labor Market Changes

Immigrant States

If we are going to comment on how immigrants affect us, we should first talk about the details of how we estimate this effect. If we wanted to measure how immigration affects natives, where would be the best place to look? One option is to look nationally—how has GDP changed, how has the national average wage rate changed, how has unemployment changed at a national level? Instead, we could look more locally, which could potentially change our results significantly since labor markets in South Dakota are probably not affected by immigration the same way that labor markets in California are affected. As it turns out, each of these approaches has its pros and cons.

There is a bit of good news if we choose to examine local labor markets—the majority of immigrants settle in only a handful of places. Approximately two-thirds of all immigrants settle in one of six states in the United States (we actually introduced these earlier—we will call these the "immigrant states")—see Table 5.2.

The states on this list are actually more obvious than it may appear at first glance—they are the states that are home to the four largest cities in the country (New York, L.A., Chicago, and Houston) plus New Jersey (which is likely on the list thanks to its proximity to New York City) and Florida (which is probably driven by its proximity to Cuba). So it's possible (although not proven) that immigrants prefer to live in states

---

[6] Hanson, "Why Does Immigration Divide America?" p. 23.

Figure 5.14[7]

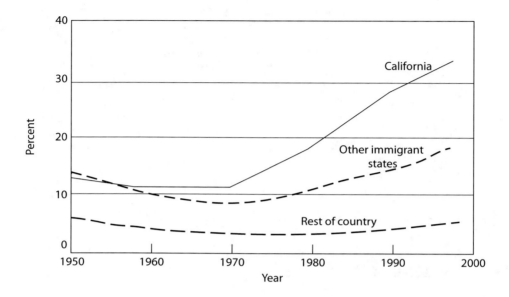

that house large metropolitan areas. A counter argument might be that large metropolitan areas develop around immigrant populations. Perhaps immigrants introduce a needed labor force for big city development, or perhaps the lower wages of immigrants is attractive to urban growth. Further it's possible that simple geographic proximity is the driving force. Since both Texas and California border Mexico, the source of most immigrants to the United States, it might simply be the case that immigrants choose to stay as close to home as possible. If this were the case, however, I would expect to see Arizona or New Mexico on the list above. Why do immigrants prefer California? Could it be the huge agricultural sector in California? This certainly contributes. (Recall that about 20% of agricultural workers are foreign-born.)

Figure 5.14 shows how these numbers have evolved over time. As we have seen, the immigration reform of 1965 resulted in a large increase in immigration, particularly from Latin American countries like Mexico. This accounts for the sharp increase in the proportion of immigrants, particularly in California.

The figure above implies that the majority of the immigrant state immigrants arrived at this time—soon after 1965. However, what is not clear is whether immigrants headed directly for their eventual destinations in the immigrant states or if there been a gradual mingling of people until their eventual settling in these locations. Essentially we're asking if the effect on local labor markets has been isolated or if it has wandered

[7] Borjas, *Heaven's Door*, p. 65.

Figure 5.15[8]

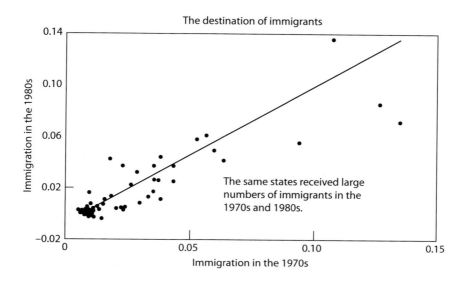

Figure 5.16[9]

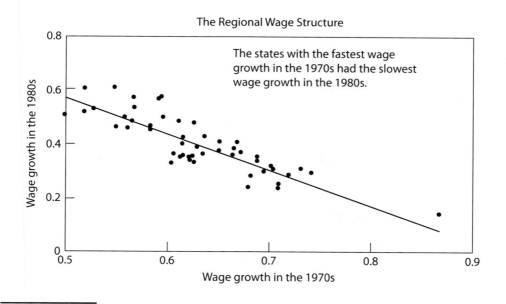

[8] Borjas, *Heaven's Door*, p. 71.

[9] Borjas, *Heaven's Door*, p. 71.

around the country over time. As the previous scatter plot shows, the destination of these immigrants has remained largely unchanged since the period of initial increase. The states that received large numbers of immigrants during the 1970s also received large numbers of immigrants during the following decade as well.

Since recently popular destinations for immigrants appear to have been popular since the policy changes in the 1960s, it follows logically that we may be able to develop an understanding of how immigrants affect wages and employment simply by looking at these six states' labor markets. Since immigrants have never gone anywhere else, how could they affect labor markets outside of the immigrant states? (I'm obviously foreshadowing here.)

Local Labor Markets

We know that the 1970s marked the beginning of an era of change due to the immigration policies of 1965. We also know that immigration should have driven up wages (if complements) or down wages (if substitutes) depending on the substitutability of immigrant labor. So let's test these theories to see if these changes in policy and the subsequent influx of immigrants had any effect on observed wages. This may not be an easy task, as the next example shows.

Figure 5.16 shows that states experiencing growing wages in the 1970s (the beginning of the influx) saw slow wage growth during the 1980s. In other words, most states were having wage growth during *either* the 1970s *or* the 1980s—not both.

What are the implications of this trend for the immigration debate? Well, we know from Figure 5.15 that the states attracting immigrants during the 1970s were still attracting them during the 1980s. If one of those states had rapid wage growth during the 1970s, we would see a positive correlation with wages and immigration—a correlation that would then be reversed during the 1980s when immigration was still high, but wage growth slowed. Thus, depending on when we studied this relationship, we could possibly conclude that immigration is positively, negatively, or not correlated with changes in the wage rate. This problem is partly caused by the fact that local effects to the labor market seldom stay local, and these are local data. We will revisit this in a later section. For now, we should use this information to prepare ourselves for the possibility that empirical evidence may be unclear.

The following table gives additional evidence of how immigration impacts native wages. The entries are percent change in the average native wage if there were to be a 10% increase in the number of immigrants. These numbers are calculated for different education levels over several decades, beginning prior to 1965.

Table 5.3[10]

	Percent change in the wage of native workers if there is one more immigrant per ten native workers					
	Men			Women		
	1960–70	1970–80	1980–90	1960–70	1970–80	1980–90
State data: All natives	5.9	0.7	–1.0	2.0	3.7	–0.2
Metropolitan area data						
High school dropouts	—	–0.7	5.7	—	–6.4	6.0
High school graduates	—	–2.6	2.2	—	1.1	7.1
Some college	—	0.2	3.7	—	0.3	6.9
Metropolitan area data, adjusted for possibility that immigrants cluster in high-wage areas						
High school dropouts	—	–8.7	9.3	—	–22.5	9.9
High school graduates	—	–7.9	8.3	—	–4.5	9.9
Some college	—	–6.3	5.9	—	–3.2	8.7

Figure 5.17[11]

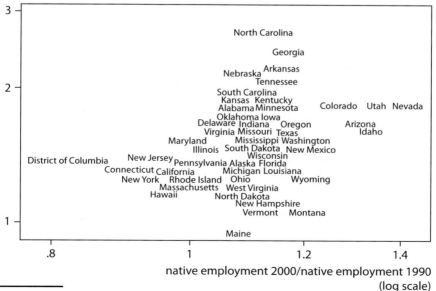

Growth in immigrant population and native employment rate, 1990 and 2000

---

[10] Figure taken from Borjas, *Heaven's Door*, p. 69.

[11] Hanson, "Why Does Immigration Divide America?" p. 24.

There are several interesting things in this table. First, it appears that prior to the policy changes in 1965, native wages were positively affected by immigrants—5.9% for men and 2% for women. This implies an early relationship of complements for the two groups. However, as time passed, both male and female native wages became negatively affected by immigration. This implies that immigrants became substitutes for native labor. This is a very interesting finding, since we have some evidence that immigrants have become less skilled over time, which implies that United States natives are also low skilled currently. This is not typically how we describe the United States labor force.

However, this trend disappears when we focus on metropolitan areas and separate the data by education level. Once we refine the data this way, it looks like most groups experienced a dip during the 1970s (implying substitutability of immigrant labor) but then recovered by the 1980s. This appears to be consistent with the notion that short-run and long-run effects are different, and that short-run reduction in wages eventually become long-run gains as capital investment increases.

Why is there such a difference between the data concerning "all natives" and the data for metropolitan areas? It's possible that rural, agricultural wages are driven down considerably by immigrant labor, which brings down the average. The change over time is consistent with this, since the average immigrant in 1960 was high skilled and the average immigrant in 1990 is low skilled, so an immigrant would complement agricultural labor in the 1960s but substitute for it in the 1990s. Also realize that the data breakdown for metropolitan areas is primarily for low education levels—"some college" is not really high skilled. So wages for low-skill labor seems to suffer in the SR and recover in the LR—very consistent with our theory.

What about unemployment? We've been concerned primarily with wage changes due to immigration, but is it possible that immigrants are displacing native workers? If so, the effect of immigration on labor markets would not be fully captured by changes in wage. Figure 5.16 is a scatter plot relating immigration and unemployment.

Don't worry about the log scale. It's there just to correct for growth trends and make sure we're comparing apples to apples. On the x-axis, we have employment in 2000 divided by employment in 1990. So points far to the right are places that experienced rapid growth in the employment rate between 1990 and 2000. On the y-axis, we have immigrant population share in 2000 divided by immigrant population share in 1990. Points higher up thus represent locations that experienced large increases in the proportion of immigrants between 1990 and 2000. If a location is high and to the right, that location is experiencing both growth in employment and immigration, while those to the lower left are experiencing slower growth in both. Although it's not necessarily a good fit, it looks like an upward sloping trend line could be fitted to this scatter plot, which means employment and immigration move in the same direction. This is evidence that immigrants do not displace native workers.

The Mariel Boatlift

In April, 1980, Fidel Castro announced that Cubans wishing to leave for the United States could do so freely from the port of Mariel. (If you're not familiar with Cuban policy, just know that leaving Cuba is a luxury most Cubans rarely experienced.) As a result, nearly 125,000 Cubans arrived in Miami over a six-month period—resulting in a 7% increase in Miami's labor supply in a very short period of time (think of it as an instantaneous increase in labor supply). By studying the effect of this massive and sudden increase in immigrant labor, we can hopefully gain some insight as to how immigrants affect local markets.

As it turns out, unemployment for white workers was down between 1979 and 1981 in both Miami and in similar comparison cities. However, in Miami, unemployment for white workers was down more than it was in other cities. Unemployment among black workers was up between 1979 and 1981 in both Miami and the comparison group of cities. However, this rate was up less in Miami than it was in the other cities (see Table 5.4).

Since the influx of immigrants coincided with a relative improvement in the labor market, the Mariel Boatlift incident appears to support the claim that immigrants and natives are complements for each other. However, as we will shortly see, it may be dangerous to have too much confidence in our conclusion that immigrants complement native labor in local markets due to the limited scope of the sample studied.

Table 5.4[12]

Immigration and the Miami Labor Market		
	The Mariel flow	
	Before (1979)	After (1981)
Unemployment rate in Miami		
Whites	5.1	3.9
Blacks	8.3	9.6
Unemployment rate in comparison cities		
Whites	4.4	4.3
Blacks	10.3	12.6

---

[12] Borjas, *Heaven's Door*, p. 72.

Figure 5.18[13]

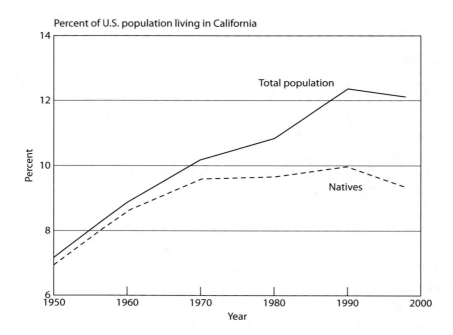

Percent of U.S. population living in California

National Labor Markets

Voting with Your Feet
We mentioned that, despite their appeal, results like that of the Mariel Boatlift may be problematic. The issue with this particular study, and many others like it, is that they focus on estimation of immigration on local labor markets. As we have seen, the majority of immigrants tend to settle in a handful of cities and states, so estimating the effect on these local markets is very appealing. However, there are some major complications with this approach, all of which can be simmered down to approximately one simple claim: *natives move.*

This claim covers movement of native labor in response to immigrant population growth, in addition to movement of native firms in response to availability of labor and the relative prices of resources. Thus, as immigrants pour into California, supplying a vast amount of relatively inexpensive low-skill labor, firms may decide to move from elsewhere in the United States to California to take advantage of this. Likewise, low-

---

[13] Borjas, *Heaven's Door*, p. 74.

Figure 5.19[14]

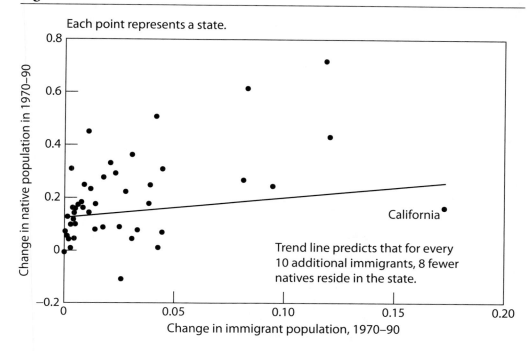

Each point represents a state.

(y-axis) Change in native population in 1970–90

(x-axis) Change in immigrant population, 1970–90

California

Trend line predicts that for every 10 additional immigrants, 8 fewer natives reside in the state.

skill native labor that once lived in California may decide to move to Iowa in response to the recent influx of competition for jobs.

This movement by native workers and firms means that the effect of immigration will not stay local to where the immigrants settle. If a firm moves from Iowa to California due to Californian immigration, then part of the effect of this immigration is carried by labor markets in Iowa since the firm's movement will reduce the number of jobs there (and presumably this will reduce the wage rate in Iowa as well). Likewise, if a native worker moves to Iowa from California, then part of the effect of immigration is carried by the labor markets in Iowa, since the supply of low-skill workers in Iowa will increase, thereby driving down wages slightly. In light of all of these changes, the labor markets in California (or in any one of the other immigrant destinations) may remain unchanged, while the bulk of the labor market impact is absorbed by Iowans. We call this movement in response to policies (in this case immigration policy) "voting with your feet."

Do we see evidence of natives voting with their feet? Do natives flee to Iowa when immigrants arrive in California? One indication that natives are responding to increases in immigration in this way would be evidence that, as immigrant population

---

[14] Figure taken from Borjas, *Heaven's Door*, p. 76.

Figure 5.20[15]

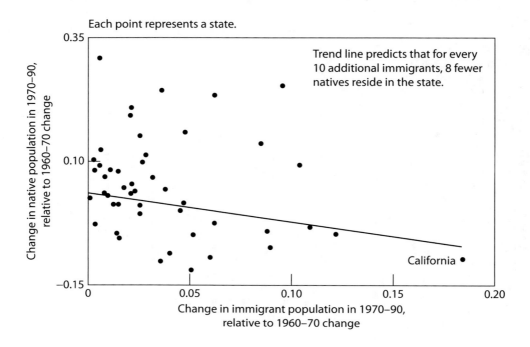

Each point represents a state.

Trend line predicts that for every 10 additional immigrants, 8 fewer natives reside in the state.

California

Change in native population in 1970–90, relative to 1960–70 change

Change in immigrant population in 1970–90, relative to 1960–70 change

increases, native population decreases. The following figure attempts to capture this for California.

California's population growth during this period of time was extraordinary, going from about 7% of the United States population in 1950 to over 12% after 1990. However, it is clear from the figure above that most of this growth was fueled by immigration growth—the native population barely changed between 1970 and 2000, and appears to have declined somewhat since 1990. However, we should take care to not misinterpret these data—it is possible that the apparent lack of native population growth was not due to immigration, but instead is due to other factors we have yet to account for. To illustrate this danger, consider the two previous figures.

The data used to construct Figures 5.19 and 5.20 start in the 1970s, which was chosen since this was the first full decade after the immigration reforms in the mid-1960s. The trend line indicates that states receiving large numbers of immigrants during this period also received large numbers of natives—indicating that natives were not obviously fleeing immigrant populations. It would appear the immigrants attract natives, or vice versa. However, we have failed to control for one simple and obvious fact: there may be a third factor that is attracting both groups. Perhaps amazing economic growth

[15] Figure taken from Borjas, *Heaven's Door*, p. 77.

is magnetic to natives *despite* the increase in immigration to that region. In other words, is it possible that the growth of native population would have been even larger if immigration growth were smaller?

We can correct for this oversight using the same set of data but approaching the problem differently. Instead of looking at population growth during 1970 to 1990, let's look at population growth during this period relative to population growth prior. Essentially we are going to look at the change in population growth.

A point far to the right in Figure 5.20 means that the state or location experienced huge post-1970s immigration and relatively small pre-1970s immigration. Points farther up in the scatter plot are for locations that experienced huge native population growth during the post-1970s era and relatively small native population growth during the pre-1970s era. Now states like California that have large immigrant population changes after the 1970s relative to the 1960s (thanks in part to the immigration reform of 1965) appear to have lower native population growth after the 1970s. The trend predicts that an increase of 10 in immigrant population results in 8 fewer natives. This implies that natives do in fact vote with their feet—they flee from areas experiencing large immigration growth.

Do all workers vote with their feet, or only low-skill workers? Immigration may not only affect the number of native workers, it may also (or instead) affect the composition of native workers. For example, if low-skill workers are fleeing from California to Iowa, is the mix of California natives becoming more skilled? As the figure below indicates, the answer may be "yes." (We have seen this figure before!)

The ratio of college graduates to high school dropouts is increasing in California and the other immigrant states at a much faster rate than the rest of the nation. We may be inclined to credit immigration for this difference, but as we will see, other factors need to be controlled for—like the fact that California's high tech industry may be growing faster than in other areas. For now, let's just say that immigration may contribute to a changing mix of native workers. (Even this claim may be a stretch, since there is no way for us to be certain what's causing the changes seen in Figure 5.21.)

It appears that native workers do in fact migrate away from areas experiencing rapid immigration growth. This is consistent with the idea that the effect of immigration will be spread out over an area larger than the local destination of immigrants—Iowa will also feel the impact of immigration.

What about firms? Do firms also relocate in response to immigration? We would expect that, if immigration drives down wages, firms would be eager to move to these areas in order to enjoy relatively cheaper labor. As the following table shows, evidence may be unclear.

Figure 5.21[16]

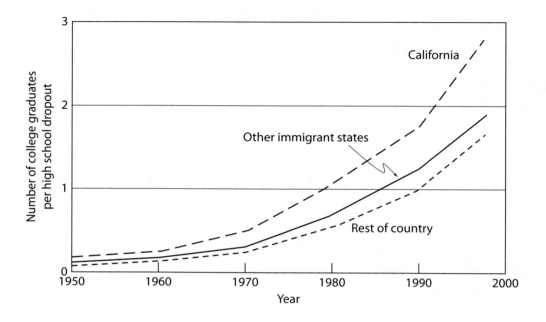

Table 5.5[17]

Employment Growth in Immigrant Industries, 1970–90

	Annual percent change in employment		
	California	Other immigrant states	Rest of country
Industries that are immigrant-intensive	2.5	1.3	1.5
Manufacturing	1.7	0.1	0.6
Personal services	2.2	1.2	0.9
Industries that are not immigrant-intensive	2.8	2.4	2.4
Professional services	3.2	2.9	2.8
Transportation, communications, and utilities	2.3	1.9	2.0

---

[16] Figure taken from Borjas, *Heaven's Door*, p. 79.

[17] Borjas, *Heaven's Door*, p. 81.

Compare the data for California to the rest of the nation. These data seem to imply that firms are in fact growing more in the locations where immigrant populations have been increasing. California has grown faster than the rest of the nation in all sectors, but those particular sectors that are considered to be immigrant-labor intensive have grown much faster in California—two or three times as fast as non-immigrant locations.

However, this compelling conclusion seems to evaporate when we consider the other five immigrant states. Although these states have almost identical growth rates as the rest of the nation, the immigrant intensive industries have grown *slower* than elsewhere (with the one exception of "personal services"). This implies that firms respond positively only to immigration in California, which is weird. (By "weird" I mean to imply that something besides immigration is probably driving some of these results.)

Although we cannot definitively conclude that firms respond to immigration from these data, we also cannot completely dismiss this idea. This evidence implies that some locations, such as California, did experience changes in industrial behavior or composition in light of immigration following the 1965 policy changes. Overall, I think we can safely say that there is some evidence to suggest that both native workers and firms respond (at least in part) to immigration the way our theories predicted—low-skill native labor leaves and low-skill-intensive firms enter. This movement of labor and firms means that the effect of immigration is spread to areas where immigrants are not. This may seem counterintuitive at first—that immigrants can affect wages in areas where they are not—but this can in fact be the case. Since this is true, our local measurements of immigration impact may be wrong (which is settling since we had some confusing results locally).

In order to cope with the fact that native workers and firms may be voting with their feet, we expand our analysis of labor markets to include the entire nation. By changing our focus from local markets to national markets, we should avoid the possible (although not definitive) pitfalls of native migration spreading the impact of immigration to places like Iowa.

On a national level, we should evaluate the claim that low-skill workers are hurt by immigration since immigrants "take our jobs" in low-skill-intensive sectors. This study has been done, and there does appear to be a significant contribution of immigration to the wage gap between high-skill and low-skill workers. A 1997 paper by George Borjas and Richard Freeman shows that 44% of the gap between high- and low-skill wages (which has increased from around 30% to over 40%) can be attributed to immigration if we define "low skill" to be high school dropouts. However, this result depends very much on how you define "low skill." Changing the definition so that low skill is equal to having a diploma as opposed to dropping out (high skill is defined as having a college degree) drastically affects the outcome—only about 5% of the gap is due to immigration in this case. This means that the wage of high school graduates was

Table 5.6[18]

The Impact of Immigration on the National Labor Market

	Definition of "unskilled" versus "skilled"	
	High school dropouts versus all other education groups	High school graduates versus college graduates
Number of unskilled immigrants who arrived between 1979 and 1995 per hundred unskilled natives	20.7	5.6
Number of skilled immigrants who arrived between 1979 and 1995 per hundred skilled natives	4.1	4.3
Percent wage differential between skilled and unskilled natives in 1979	30.1%	30.4%
Percent wage differential between skilled and unskilled natives in 1995	41.0%	49.5%
Percent of the change in the wage gap between skilled and unskilled natives attributable to immigration	44.0%	4.7%

barely affected by immigration. These results are summarized in Table 5.6.

Table 5.6 shows that between 1979 and 1995, there was about a 17% relative increase in low-skill immigrants. This is found by taking the increase in low-skill immigrants during this period (about 20.7%) and subtracting the increase in high-skill immigrants (4.1%). As for the wage gap, we saw a change from 30.1% to 41%—about an 11% difference. Of this, 44% is due to immigrants, which turns out to be about 5%. Thus, it is estimated that this 17% relative increase in unskilled immigrants lowered the wage of native high school dropouts by about 5%.

So what should we take with us from all of this discussion of immigration and labor markets? It seems clear that immigration does affect wages. More specifically, immigration drives down wages for low-skilled workers. The degree of this effect is unclear and depends on things like our definition of "low skill" (the lower the skill level is, the bigger the drop in wage will be), as well as how specific the geographical region we are examining is. It also seems clear that native workers and firms respond to immigration

---

[18] Borjas, *Heaven's Door*, p. 83.

by moving around the country. It appears workers flee from and firms flock toward immigrants. The degree to which this migration affects labor markets is not entirely clear. There is one thing we can be very certain of: the impact of immigration on labor markets is, at best, difficult to measure and changes over time—the SR effects may be very different from the LR effects.

So in general we can confidently say in which direction immigration pushes labor markets, but we have a hard time saying anything about how big this push is.

Chapter 6

Non-labor Impacts of Immigration

Costs and Benefits of Immigration

Recent issues, including things like the legislation in Arizona, have fueled the debate about the costs and benefits of immigration. Angry natives want immigration controlled (or stopped in some cases), and advocates for immigration argue for immigrant rights. In a recent survey of United States residents, 70% of high school dropouts said that immigration should be decreased from its present level (only 48% of college graduates shared this view). What drives this response? (I assure you it isn't the average American's intimate knowledge of the economics behind the immigration issue.) As we have seen, immigration's impact on labor markets is, although existent, by no means straightforward. So why do the vast majority of United States residents have such strong opinion about immigration policy? Should we want to keep immigrants out?

As economists, we can fortunately put aside all aspects of this debate that revolve around the humanitarian aspect of immigration and immigrant rights. Claims like "immigrants are people too" are irrelevant to what we will do here. (They are people, by the way.) Instead, we will try to quantify the impact of immigration on society. Part of this impact is the effect immigration has on wages and employment. We know immigration drives down low-skill wages in the SR. This in turn makes goods and services cheaper for native consumers. Interestingly, the fact that immigration drives down wages turns out to be crucial for the existence of social gain from immigration. The fact that native firms pay workers less, and this cost reduction is passed on to consumers in the form of lower prices, drives the result that society as a whole may be better off with immigration than without.

However, this is only part of the story. Immigrants also shop at the grocery store, they buy gasoline and clothes, and they use services like dentists and the post office. This consumption means more money in the hands of native firms and entrepreneurs (and in the hands of immigrant entrepreneurs, too). These entrepreneurs in turn spend this money on everything from workers to beers, and so on, rippling through the economy. There are other external benefits of immigration to consider too—things like delicious cuisine and cultural diversity that would be noticeably absent without

Homeland Security Scraps Border Fence

By Keith Johnson
Wall Street Journal, January 15, 2011

The Department of Homeland Security Friday pulled the plug on a troubled billion-dollar program to build a high-tech fence along the Arizona border to help fight illegal immigration, a definitive end to a long-moribund project.

By scrapping the controversial SBInet program, DHS will now turn to a mix of proven, existing technology it says will help agents patrol a much bigger chunk of the Southwest border at a lower cost.

"SBInet cannot meet its original objective of providing a single, integrated border-security technology solution," Homeland Security Janet Napolitano said. She said the new solution, which will include mobile surveillance systems, unmanned aircraft and thermal-imaging devices, was "tailored to the unique needs of each border region" and would provide a "more effective balance between cost and capability."

DHS has spent the past year reviewing the program, initially conceived in 2005, which has been plagued by technology problems, cost overruns and delays. Only 53 miles of the Arizona border have been protected with SBInet technology at a cost of nearly $1 billion. In contrast, the new plan envisions covering the rest of the Arizona border—some 323 miles—for roughly $750 million.

Ms. Napolitano froze funding for the program—and its primary contractor, Boeing Corp.—in March while the assessment was being carried out.

DHS said it would continue to use some elements of the old SBInet system "that have proven successful, such as stationary radar and infrared and optical sensor towers."

Boeing said that "we appreciate that they recognize the value of the integrated fixed towers Boeing has built, tested and delivered so far," adding that "Boeing remains committed to providing valuable solutions and supporting DHS."

DHS will carry out further assessments on the southern border to determine which technologies will best help border-patrol agents detect illegal crossings.

SBInet's demise was applauded by some key members of Congress, and even critics of the administration's approach to the border didn't challenge the move.

Sen. Joe Lieberman, an independent from Connecticut who chairs the Senate Committee on Homeland Security, said in a statement that the "long-troubled" program was "unrealistic," and called the department's new plan a "far wiser approach."

New York Republican Peter King, chairman of the House Committee on Homeland Security, said: "While I understand the Department of Homeland Security decision to end the SBInet program, I continue to have very serious concerns about the Obama administration's lack of urgency to secure the border."

The administration deported a record number of illegal immigrants—more than 390,000—in the year ended Sept. 30. About half had a criminal record, in line with the administration's decision to target illegal immigrants with criminal convictions.

immigrant populations. Although it is important to recognize that these things may not be viewed as benefits by everyone—in fact these may be external costs to some.

One striking example of (probably unarguably beneficial) externalities of immigration is seen in the performance of some outstanding people in the United States who were born outside the United States. For example, the CEO of Intel (Hungarian), the CEO of Borland International and Time's Man of the Year (French), and a late CEO of Coca-Cola (Cuban). In addition, a large percentage of American Nobel Prizes are earned by immigrants: 31% in economics, 26% in chemistry, 32% in physics, and 31% in medicine.[1] Admittedly these are special cases, but the argument can easily be made that the benefits of immigration do in fact include some extraordinary feats by some outstanding individuals.

Lastly, we must consider the cost of immigrant consumption of public goods like welfare, education, and healthcare. The idea that immigrants don't pay their way is a central concern for many people involved in the immigration debate. (Interestingly, we wouldn't have to look hard to find natives who don't pay their way.) Obviously if a person consumes public goods and does not contribute via taxes to the funding of these goods, other people must bear the burden of their free-riding. What, if any, is the cost of this free-ridership? Are immigrants really different from natives in this regard?

One danger in facing issues concerning the costs and benefits of immigration is separating oneself from personal beliefs and emotional involvement in these matters. (This may be easier for economists, since we don't have feelings.) We cannot break down economic arguments and reasoning into a debate fueled by bigotry. A superficial glance at some of the arguments made by people involved in the debates over some of these issues reveals that people tend to be guilty of bigotry-based arguments. Please think like an economist. If economic reasoning leads you to vote against immigration,

---

[1] James P. Smith and Barry Edmonston, (1997), *The New Americans: Economic, Demographic, and Fiscal Effects of Immigration*, National Academies Press, Ch. 4, pp.135–146, 151–153.

so be it. At least there was a logical reason for your vote. The article on page 127 shows how easy it may be to forget to think like an economist (said over a plate of enchiladas…).

Immigration Surplus

The term "immigration surplus" is not intended to imply that there is an excess supply of immigration. The "surplus" is the same as when we talk about consumer surplus or producer surplus. Thus, immigration surplus is the term we give the amount of social welfare that results from immigration. The source of this surplus is as we described above—lower wages benefit firms and lower prices benefit consumers. The size of this surplus, much like the size of CS and PS, depends in part on the elasticity of labor supply.

The numbers in Table 5.6 imply that, thanks to immigration, the number of unskilled workers was up approximately 21% during the 1980s and 1990s. Likewise, skilled labor was up approximately 4% during the same period. (I am using the numbers from the left column, where unskilled is defined as high school dropout.) The difference is 17%—that is a 17% increase in the ratio of unskilled to skilled workers. As the ratio of skilled to unskilled workers changes, so must the relative wages. How much wages change is determined by the relative wage elasticity, which has been estimated to be approximately -0.32.[2] This means that a 1% increase in the proportion of unskilled labor (relative to skilled labor) results in a 0.32% reduction in unskilled wages. So, assuming an elasticity of -0.32 and a 17% increase in the proportion of unskilled workers, unskilled native wages should fall by approximately 5%.

This wage reduction obviously results in a welfare reduction for that particular group of low-skill workers. However, the story doesn't end there. Everybody who isn't in this particular group, including firms and high-skilled workers, and all consumers (including the low-skilled) benefit due to lower costs and lower prices. This means that immigration is a transfer of welfare from the poor to the wealthy. It follows that anybody who is anti-welfare should be pro-immigration.

---

[2] Borjas, George J., Richard B. Freeman and Lawrence F. Katz, (1997), "How Much Do Immigration and Trade Affect Labor Market Outcomes?" Brookings Papers on Economic Activity, 1997, pp. 1–67.

Border Fight Creeps North

A Proposed Crackdown on Illegal Immigration Divides Nebraska Farm Town

By Lauren Etter

Wall Street Journal, June 18, 2010

Fremont, Neb.—A vote Monday brings to a head a two-year battle over immigration that has divided residents here.

The split over a proposed city ordinance to crack down on illegal immigration has spilled over into churches, coffee shops and grocery stores in this agricultural center 35 miles northwest of Omaha—a long way from the U.S.–Mexico border.

Public officials in the once-homogeneous city of 25,000 have been asked not to speak on the topic, casting an odd veil of silence over the city. Mayor Donald "Skip" Edwards declined to be interviewed, saying only that "I'm not going to put myself in a difficult spot."

"The mentality and the atmosphere has changed here," said Michelle Knapp, a resident and vocal opponent of the ordinance, sitting at a quaint Main Street coffee shop. "It's fear."

Fremont's special election follows on the heels of a strict law signed by Arizona Gov. Jan Brewer making it a state crime to be in the country illegally.

While immigration has long been the purview of the federal government, states and cities like Fremont are increasingly taking matters into their own hands in the absence of a comprehensive overhaul of U.S. immigration policy.

"If you're having flooding, you're not going to wait for the federal government to sandbag," said Jerry Hart, a resident and lead proponent of the Fremont ordinance.

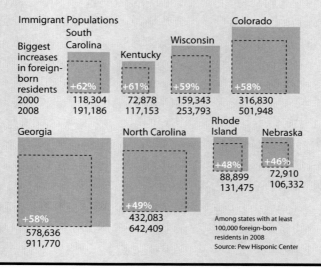

Immigrant Populations

Biggest increases in foreign-born residents

	2000	2008
South Carolina	+62%	118,304 / 191,186
Kentucky	+61%	72,878 / 117,153
Wisconsin	+59%	159,343 / 253,793
Colorado	+58%	316,830 / 501,948
Georgia	+58%	578,636 / 911,770
North Carolina	+49%	432,083 / 642,409
Rhode Island	+48%	88,899 / 131,475
Nebraska	+46%	72,910 / 106,332

Among states with at least 100,000 foreign-born residents in 2008

Source: Pew Hisponic Center

Since its founding in 1856, Fremont has been almost all white, with many residents of Swedish and German descent. Over the years, big meatpacking companies like Hormel Foods moved to town as the industry was consolidating and being pushed from urban centers to the rural Midwest. In the 1990s, the area's Hispanic population began to grow.

Today, about 1,100 immigrants, including some who lack proper documentation, call Fremont home, according to the Pew Hispanic Center, a nonpartisan research group. Manicured lawns, lilac bushes and restaurants like the Nifty Fifties are now punctuated by Mexican restaurants and tiny tiendas that sell yucca and plantains.

In June 2008, a now-retired city council member proposed an ordinance that would prohibit harboring, hiring or renting to undocumented immigrants. It would give local police more power to inquire into a person's immigration status.

The following month, residents packed the Fremont High school to debate the issue. In a vote the night of the debate, the city council split four-to-four on the proposal. Mayor Edwards cast the tie-breaking vote against the ordinance, saying he had consulted with the Nebraska attorney general and determined that immigration matters should remain in federal hands.

Disappointed by the outcome, proponents gathered more than 3,000 signatures to put the issue on a ballot for a special election. The city sued in state court, saying the ordinance would be unconstitutional. In April, the Nebraska Supreme Court concluded the measure should be put before voters.

Out-of-state groups have joined the fight. Kris Kobach, an attorney and law professor from Missouri, has been lending legal advice to Fremonters who want the ordinance. Mr. Kobach has also helped other small cities pass similar ordinances, and he helped write the Arizona law.

On the other side, the Nebraska affiliate of the American Civil Liberties Union has threatened to sue if the ordinance passes. Opponents warn that passage would lead to costly litigation the city can't afford.

After the city council vote in vote in 2008, tensions escalated. Some started calling Fremont "Frexico" and accused immigrants of bringing gang activity and disease to town. Alfredo Velez owner of Tienda Mexicana Guerrero, said somebody shot out his front window with a BB gun.

Backers of the ordinance say it will protect Fremont from becoming a "safe-haven for illegal aliens," according to a flier with an American flag being distributed across town.

Ordinance backer Edward Robinson, a farmer who lives just outside Fremont, said over a plate of enchiladas at a local Mexican restaurant that he applauds Fremont for taking action because the U.S.–Mexico border "is a portal that is so dangerous today."

Other residents, including immigrants, say the proposal would make Fremont one of America's least welcoming towns.

Earlier this week, a group of Fremont residents in a newly formed group, One Fremont One Future, gathered about 200 people in a grassy park to show their opposition to the ordinance.

The Fremont Area Chamber of Commerce recently passed a resolution opposing the proposed ordinance, saying it would impose high costs on businesses that they can ill-afford, "especially in this uncertain economy."

The city said in a fact sheet the ordinance would cost Fremont at least $1 million a year to implement and enforce. The city also said it would likely have to raise taxes and cut jobs to pay for the increases.

"It's the wrong solution," said longtime resident Don Hinds, owner of a commercial investment business in the city. It would be a "tremendous burden on landlords, city officials and the police department."

There is a diagram that follows this story. For simplicity, let's assume the supply of labor is perfectly inelastic. Nothing that follows requires this assumption, but it will make the math much easier. Immigration will shift the supply curve for labor to the right, reflecting the fact that immigrants and low-skill labor are substitutes for each other. As a result, the equilibrium wage falls, as illustrated in Figure 6.1.

There were L natives employed, and then a number equal to $L' - L$ of immigrants entered. Since the height of the demand curve represents the value of labor, the area under the demand curve (labeled MRP) up to L is the total value of labor in the economy prior to immigration (areas A + B + C before the supply shift). However, this is not how much we pay the labor. Instead, we pay only up to the wage of w, for a total amount of $w \cdot L$ (areas B + C). After the supply shift, wage drops to w'. The amount of surplus now increases to the sum of areas A + B + C + D + E. Remove from this the money paid to natives (area C) and the money paid to immigrants (area D). Area B is a transfer from native low-skill workers to consumers, and area E is new surplus, thanks to immigrants shopping, et cetera. You can think of this area as the change

Figure 6.1

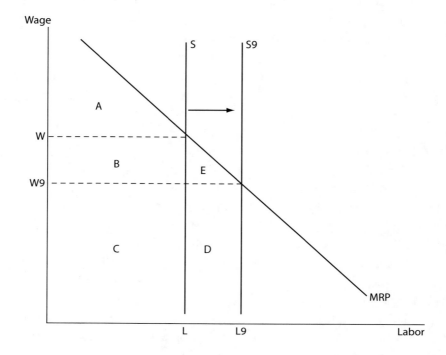

in GDP (call it ΔY) thanks to immigration. This area, area E, is what we will try to estimate next.

The area labeled E in the diagram above is approximately equal to one half base times height, or:

$$\triangle Y \approx \frac{1}{2}(w - w')(L' - L).$$

Notice that the demand and supply curves need not be exactly linear, which is why I said "approximately equal to"—to allow for non-linear (but almost linear) demand. The amount $(L' - L)$ is exactly equal to the amount of immigration. In order to keep the primes in the same order, I want to switch the order of the w and w' within the first set of parentheses to get:

$$\triangle Y \approx -\frac{1}{2}(w' - w)(L' - L).$$

The only difference now is that there is a negative sign in front and the prime term is always first. As long as the demand curve for labor is almost linear, we can write the following:

$$(w' - w) \approx \left(\frac{\Delta w}{\Delta L}\right)(L' - L),$$

This is essentially defining the slope of the demand curve. If we substitute this into the previous equation for ΔY, we get:

$$\Delta Y \approx -\frac{1}{2}\left[\left(\frac{\Delta w}{\Delta L}\right)(L' - L)\right](L' - L),$$

where the stuff inside the square brackets is the substitution we made. Just for fun, let's divide both sides by Y (it's obviously not just for fun, but the reason may not be clear at this point—we'll need to have Y in the denominator for what comes next):

$$\frac{\Delta Y}{Y} \approx -\frac{1}{2} \cdot \frac{1}{Y} \cdot \left[\left(\frac{\Delta w}{\Delta L}\right)(L' - L)\right](L' - L).$$

It looks messy now, but we'll clean this up in a second. For now, pay attention to the fact that on the left-hand side of the equal sign, we have the change in GDP that is due to immigration, in percentage terms. I want to replace both ($L' - L$) with the capital letter M (which stands for immigration, since ($L' - L$) is the amount of immigration), and get rid of the square brackets:

$$\frac{\Delta Y}{Y} \approx -\frac{1}{2} \cdot \frac{1}{Y} \cdot \left(\frac{\Delta w}{\Delta L}\right)M \cdot M.$$

The term inside the parentheses on the right side looks almost like elasticity—but not quite. Recall that elasticity is

$$\frac{\Delta Q / Q}{\Delta P / P} = \frac{\Delta Q}{\Delta P} \cdot \frac{P}{Q}$$

so what we're missing inside the parentheses is a term that looks like this: $\frac{L}{w}$ So let's put it there, but if we do, then the equality will no longer hold. (We can't just multiply the right side of an equation by $\frac{L}{w}$ unless we do the same to the left side!) To get

around this, we multiply the right side by $\frac{L}{w}$ and at the same time divide the right side

by $\frac{L}{w}$ (or multiply by $\frac{w}{L}$). This is a shortcut that is equivalent to multiplying the right side by 1 so that the equality is unaffected. So, we will have:

$$\frac{L}{w} \cdot \frac{\Delta Y}{Y} \approx -\frac{1}{2} \cdot \frac{1}{Y} \cdot \left(\frac{\Delta w}{\Delta L} \cdot \frac{L}{w}\right) M \cdot M,$$

and now multiply both sides by $\frac{w}{L}$ to get

$$\frac{\Delta Y}{Y} \approx -\frac{1}{2} \cdot \frac{1}{Y} \cdot \left(\frac{\Delta w}{\Delta L} \cdot \frac{L}{w}\right) M \cdot M \cdot \frac{w}{L}$$

Repeat this procedure one more time, but this time multiply and divide the right side by L. (At this point you're wondering what the hell is going on, right? Just bear with me, we need to have the correct terms on the right side so that the interpretation makes sense. This repeated multiplying and dividing allows me to introduce variables without ruining the equality.)

$$\frac{\Delta Y}{Y} \approx -\frac{1}{2} \cdot \frac{1}{Y} \cdot \left(\frac{\Delta w}{\Delta L} \cdot \frac{L}{w}\right) M \cdot M \cdot \frac{w}{L} \cdot L \cdot \frac{1}{L}$$

Now group terms:

$$\frac{\Delta Y}{Y} \approx -\frac{1}{2} \cdot \frac{wL}{Y} \cdot \left(\frac{\Delta w}{\Delta L} \frac{L}{w}\right) \frac{M}{L} \frac{M}{L}.$$

Ok, now we can talk about what this says. Keep in mind that is merely an expression for the area of the triangle in the earlier diagram—it estimates the percent change

of GDP that is due to immigration. The term $\frac{wL}{Y}$ is the total amount of money paid to labor (wL) divided by total GDP (Y). So this is the percent of GDP that is wages—this is labor's share of GDP. (Let's call this term *s* for labor's "share" of GDP.) The term

inside the parentheses, $\frac{\Delta w}{\Delta L} \frac{L}{w}$, is the inverse of elasticity. Yes, this is the inverse of

elasticity—it is $\frac{1}{e}$. To see this, revisit the formula for elasticity of demand: $\frac{\Delta Q}{\Delta P} \cdot \frac{P}{Q}$. The

ΔQ is in the numerator, and Q is on the x-axis of the demand curve graph. Likewise, for the labor demand graph, L is on the x-axis, so elasticity should have ΔL in the numerator—but it appears in the denominator in our term. Thus, this term is equal to $\frac{1}{e}$, which is the amount (in % terms) that wages fall if labor increases by 1%. Lastly, the term $\frac{M}{L}$ is the share of the labor force that is immigrants. I will abbreviate this with a lowercase m for immigration share of the labor force.

So, using the abbreviations described in the last paragraph, we can rewrite our formula for percent change in GDP due to immigration as:

$$\frac{\Delta Y}{Y} \approx -\frac{1}{2}s\left(\frac{1}{e}\right)m^2.$$

Estimating these quantities is no easy task. In the United States, labor's share of GDP is about 70%. This is fairly well known. As for the portion of the labor force that is composed of immigrant labor, although there is some debate (thanks in part to un-documented workers, among other things), estimates put this at about 10%. Elasticity of demand for labor can take on a wide variety of values. The dispersion can be due to a number of factors including which industry you consider and if you estimate long-run or short-run elasticity. Here, we are concerned primarily with low-skill industries in the short run, since these will be most impacted by immigration. In an earlier section of this text, we saw that a 17% relative increase in low-skilled immigrants resulted in a 5% reduction in low-skill native wages. It follows that a 1% increase in low-skill immigration will result in a drop in low-skill native wages by 0.3%—i.e.,

$$\frac{\%\Delta w}{\%\Delta L} = \frac{1}{e} = -0.3.$$

Plugging these numbers into the equation above gives us the following:

$$\frac{\Delta Y}{Y} \approx -\frac{1}{2}(.7)(-.3)(.1^2) = 0.1\%.$$

So, in the United States, given our current values for s, $\frac{1}{e}$ and m, we see that immigration increases GDP by about 0.1%. Given our current GDP of about $14 trillion, this amounts to an increase of $14 billion.

It is important to realize that changing the estimates of elasticity of the proportion of the labor force that is immigrants may drastically change this $14 billion estimate. For example, some studies have found that elasticity of labor is in the ballpark of .4 to .5, and if we use these numbers (I'll use the average of .45), we get a surplus around

Figure 6.2

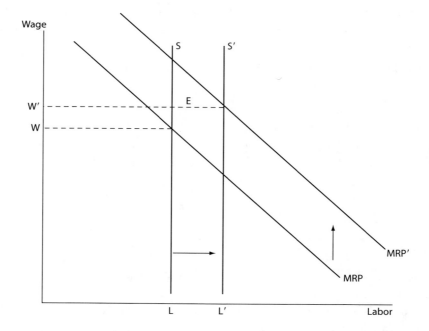

$100 billion instead of $14 billion. This is no small difference, and the thought that this estimate may trickle down and eventually have policy implications is a bit unsettling given our lack of confidence in this number.

One additional key assumption throughout this is that the amount of immigration affects only the amount of labor and not the amount of capital in the economy. This was illustrated by a shift of only the supply curve for labor—the demand curve did not shift. If we allow the amount of capital to change in addition, the diagram will look something like the one shown in Figure 6.2. Notice that the surplus remains, but the decrease in total wages paid to natives caused by immigration is lessened.

Despite the potential problems with this framework, we can make some interesting conclusions about the impact of immigration on the United States social welfare. First, notice that, despite our varying estimates of elasticity, the sign on the surplus is positive. This means that immigration benefits society. Remember how—essentially because goods get cheaper because wages fall. This brutal fact is the only thing that drives the result that immigration benefits society. Unfortunately, any benefit comes at the cost of our own low-skill native workers. Harvard Professor George Borjas, in his book *Heaven's Door* (from which I have pulled much of this material) summarized this harsh reality nicely:

> Many participants in the immigrant debate often argue that there is no evidence whatsoever that immigrants harm the employment opportunities of

Figure 6.3

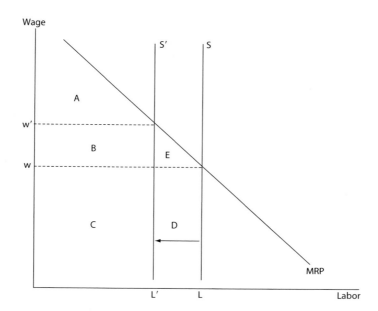

native workers. The Urban Institute's attempt at "setting the record straight," for example, concludes that "immigration has no discernible effect on wages overall…. Wage growth and decline appear to be unrelated to immigration." And the late Julian Simon's "interpretation of the literature" is that there is only "a minor negative effect."

Ironically, those who typically take this stand are often the ones who stress the beneficial aspects of immigration, and who advocate a more open immigration policy. They are in for a shock: *there is no immigration surplus if the native wage is not reduced by immigration*. In other words, if some workers are not harmed by immigration, many of the benefits that are typically attributed to immigration—higher profits for firms, lower prices for consumers—cease to exist. As I pointed out earlier, no pain, no gain.

Overall, if you can take only one thing with you from this discussion, I think it should be this: the impact of immigration is positive and relatively small. A $14 billion surplus (or even a $100 billion surplus for that matter) is not profound when you are talking about a 14 trillion dollar GDP. It is much less than 1% of GDP. Even on the high end of estimates of this surplus ($100 billion), this amounts to about $200 to $300 per person, per year.

Figure 6.4

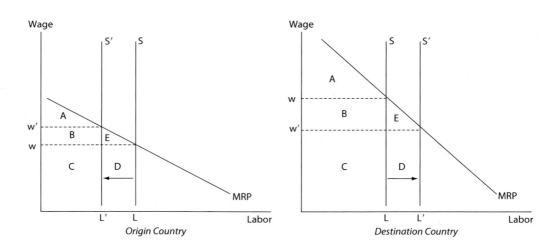

Origin Country   Destination Country

What about labor markets in the country where the immigrant labor originated? How does their departure affect wages and surplus there? A similar diagram illustrates this effect, as shown in Figure 6.3.

Since people are leaving the country, the supply of labor shifts left and the prevailing wage increases. As a result of the higher wage (and thus higher costs), consumers suffer and must give up areas B and E. For the workers, total wage income falls by D, but then immediately increases by B (this was C + D prior to the migration, C + B after). Thus, after the dust settles, change in surplus due to emigration is negative, and is equal to area E.

You might be tempted to think that, since the destination country gains an area E and the origin country loses an area E, the world consisting of only these two countries is exactly the same after the labor movement. However, the MRP curve of the destination country probably isn't in the same place as the MRP curve for the origin country. The same is true for the supply labor curve. More specifically, it's probable that the MRP curve for the destination country is higher than that of the origin country (resulting in higher wages and thus the incentive to relocate). People are less likely to relocate to a country where productivity is lower. This means the area gained by the destination country is going to be larger than the area lost by the origin country, even though from far away they may look the same. Figure 6.4 illustrates this.

So, how do we feel overall about immigration's effect on social surplus? It turns out that immigration is a transfer from workers to consumers (or from workers to firm owners) and it is a transfer from the origin country to the destination country. So who gains the most? Consumers and firms in the destination country do. Who loses the most? Consumers and firm owners in the origin country do.

Chapter 7

Public Goods, Welfare and Immigration

Do Immigrants Free-ride?

Free-riding is the process of using public goods without contributing to cover the cost of their provision. Typically, we all contribute to public good provision via taxes. I think the argument that immigrants free-ride is frequently made on the assumption that they don't pay income taxes. It might be true that illegal immigrants don't pay income taxes, and income taxes pay for lots of things, but there are other forms of taxes and not all immigrants are illegal. In addition, there are plenty of tax-evading natives who also consume public goods. The question is "how does free-riding enter the immigration debate?"

Take the article that follows for example. California law states that any person satisfying "residency requirements" is entitled to in-state tuition—even if the person is in the country illegally. Some students filed suit, but the court ruled that the wording of California's law does not rule out illegal immigrants, so California must extend the benefit of in-state tuition to these students. Is this an example of free-riding? I want you to think carefully about how natives contribute to the funding of California schools, and consider if illegal immigrants do the same.

Notice the line in the last paragraph of the first column that reads, "Supporters of the law say it is in the state's best interest to give higher-education access to all California residents." What do you think about this? Even if issues like this don't fire you up one way or the other, hopefully you see the importance of the debate. (This is probably painfully obvious to any California students in light of recent fee increases—or for any California professors in light of recent pay cuts!)

Immigration and Welfare

Probably one of the biggest free-riding complaints concerns immigrants' use of the United States' welfare system. The idea that "immigrants don't pay their way" or that they withdraw from the system without paying into it is a major issue for many people. As Table 7.1 indicates, there may be some traction to this argument. Immigrant

Immigrants Win on College Fees

By Stu Woo
Wall Street Journal, November 16, 2010

Illegal immigrants in California may continue to pay the lower in-state fees at public colleges and universities, the state's top court ruled Monday, a decision that saves them as much as $23,000 year.

The case was closely watched by several other states, including New York and Texas, which have similar laws that allow illegal immigrants to pay in-state tuition. California residents technically pay no tuition to attend public colleges and universities, but instead pay fees that are the equivalent of tuition.

California's legislature in 2001 passed a law that let nonresidents attend state colleges at the in-state rate if they, among other things, attended a high school in California for at least three years.

At University of California institutions the in-state fee is about $12,000 a year, and the out-of-state rate is $35,000. Students at California State University schools pay an in-state fee of about $5,000 a year, compared an out-of-state rate of roughly $13,000.

A group of out-of-state students at California colleges, represented by Kansas lawyer Kris Kobach, in 2005 sued the University of California over the law. The plaintiffs said the law discriminated against out-of-state students and violated a federal prohibition against giving educational benefits to illegal immigrants, but not U.S. residents.

A lower California court ruled in favor of the plaintiffs in 2008, striking down the law, but the illegal immigrants have continued to pay the lower in-state fee since then because the ruling wasn't enforced while the appeal was pending.

The 2008 ruling was unanimously overturned Monday by the California Supreme Court. In his decision, Justice Ming Chin wrote that the California legislation didn't conflict with federal law because U.S. residents could still qualify for reduced rates even if they lived out of state, provided they attended high school in California for three years.

Mr. Kobach said Monday that he planned to appeal the decision to the U.S. Supreme Court.

The case colored the California governor's race. Republican Meg Whitman opposed granting illegal immigrants in-state rates for college while Democrat Jerry Brown, who won the election, favored giving them the lower rate.

Table 7.1[1]

Participation in Public Assistance Programs, 1998

	Percent participating in program	
	Native households	Immigrant households
Cash programs		
Public assistance or welfare	3.8	5.7
Supplemental Security Income	4.1	5.6
Noncash programs		
Energy assistance	2.7	1.9
Food stamps	7.6	10.3
Housing assistance	4.7	6.0
Medicaid	13.1	20.3
Any type of assistance	15.4	22.4

households are more likely to participate in assistance programs—22% of immigrant households compared to 15% of native households.

As with most things, a simple glance at a table doesn't tell the whole story. These numbers tell us the percent of households that are receiving aid—this does not tell us anything about how long the households receive aid or how much aid they receive. Also, recall that the immigrant population comprises about 10% of United States, so even though a smaller percentage of native households participate in assistance programs, the total number of natives receiving aid far exceeds the total number of immigrants. For example, there may be 10 million immigrant households (2.24 million on welfare) compared with 126 million native households (19.4 million on welfare). If these numbers are accurate, there are almost 10 times as many native households on welfare. In the other direction, however, is the fact that immigrant households tend to be larger than native households. For example, according to the Census Bureau, the average non-Hispanic household has 2.5 people, while the average Hispanic household has 3.5 people.[2]

What we can say is this: the probability that a randomly selected immigrant household receives aid is greater than the probability that a randomly selected native household receives aid. We cannot say that immigrants consume more welfare than natives—this is not true, simply because there are so many natives. However, as

---

[1] *Heaven's Door*, p. 109.

[2] I know that not all Hispanic households are immigrant households, but recently the majority of immigrants have been Hispanic, so these data are still informative.

Figure 7.1[3]

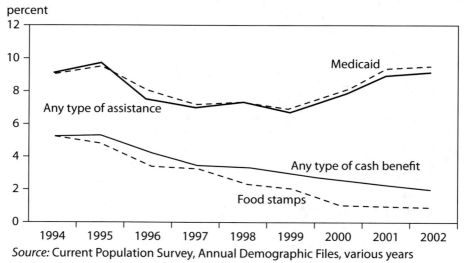

Nationwide difference in immigrant and native welfare-participation rated, 1994–2002

Source: Current Population Survey, Annual Demographic Files, various years

Figures 7.1 and 7.2 indicate, the trend of welfare consumption over time shows differences between natives and immigrants as well. The first shows the difference between immigrant and native households' consumption of various types of aid. (The y-axis measures immigrant minus native, so positive numbers imply immigrants' consumption is higher than natives'.)

The two downward sloping lines for "any type of cash benefit" and "food stamps" imply that immigrant households are more likely to consume than natives (notice the positive values on the y-axis) but the difference has been shrinking. The other two lines are similar in that immigrant households are more likely to consume these types of aid, but the difference has been growing over time.

Figure 7.2[4]

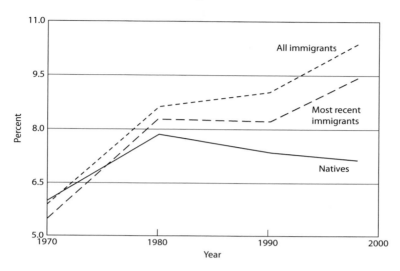

Percent of households receiving cash benefits

The plot thickens if we consider how a single household's consumption of aid changes over time, which is not shown in Figure 7.1. Do you think immigrants need assistance upon arrival and then slowly reduce their consumption of aid as they assimilate? Or, is it the case that immigrants learn about the welfare system after arriving and so the propensity to use assistance programs increases with duration of stay? Can we pull an answer out of Figure 7.2?

The distance between the lines labeled "Most recent immigrants" and "All immigrants" gets larger over time, which seems to indicate that the most recent immigrants (newest arrivals) are slightly less likely to receive assistance than those immigrants who arrived a long time ago. This implies that welfare consumption may actually increase as an immigrant assimilates.

There are also significant differences in assistance based on country of origin, both in total consumption and in duration of consumptions. For example, 37% of immigrants from the former USSR received some sort of aid upon arrival to the United States, but that number fell to 20% after 10 years in the country. Countries from Africa exhibit the opposite trend—consumption tended to increase after 10 years (see Table 7.2).

---

[4] Borjas, *Heaven's Door*, p. 107.

Table 7.2[5]

Country of birth	Percent of households receiving some type of assistance	Percent of households receiving some type of assistance after ten years in the United States
Europe		
Germany	7.8	7.8
Greece	10.4	10.2
Ireland	5.8	5.6
Italy	12.9	13.3
Poland	7.8	6.8
Portugal	16.8	18.0
USSR	37.1	20.7
United Kingdom	9.7	9.5
Asia		
Cambodia	47.9	46.6
China	17.5	19.4
India	5.6	5.6
Japan	9.7	8.6
Korea	17.3	22.3
Laos	59.1	46.0
Philippines	13.4	13.2
Vietnam	28.7	22.8
Americas		
Canada	9.9	11.7
Cuba	30.7	28.6
Dominican Republic	54.9	58.0
El Salvador	25.2	25.9
Haiti	20.2	19.4
Jamaica	22.7	19.3
Mexico	34.1	33.6
Africa		
Egypt	16.2	20.5
Nigeria	25.7	32.8

Differences in Welfare Use Among National Origin Groups, 1998

Explanations for the increased propensity to receive aid include differences in education, skill level, the number and composition of family members in a household, and the circumstances under which they have migrated. This is particularly true when we consider immigrants classified as refugees. Almost 29% of refugee households consumed some type of assistance, compared to 21% of non-refugee immigrant households and only 15% of native households. This difference is due to the fact that United States policies provide additional opportunity for aid to refugees (they are refugees, after all). This amounted to about $400 million via the refugee resettlement program. Interestingly, age seems to play little role in determining who consumes public aid—households that contain a person over the age of 65 have the same propensity

[5] Borjas, *Heaven's Door*, p. 110.

Table 7.3

Summary of aid expenditure in the United States

Year	Current dollars	2000 dollars	Medical benefits	Cash aid	Food benefits	Housing benefits	Education benefits	Jobs/ training	Services	Energy aid
1980	105,312	224,866	69,606	61,332	28,924	21,869	11,052	18,589	9,818	3,675
1985	144,291	231,158	79,204	60,294	32,666	24,207	15,972	6,370	8,773	3,672
1990	213,055	282,815	115,250	72,019	33,326	23,926	19,102	5,631	11,267	2,294
1993	314,451	374,152	170,155	89,003	43,237	32,672	17,941	6,346	12,889	1,909
1994	352,487	408,624	187,153	100,067	43,909	34,142	18,015	6,393	16,633	2,311
1995	371,109	418,484	196,922	103,291	43,558	35,764	18,146	6,132	12,775	1,896
1996	375,310	411,725	195,199	101,426	42,876	35,656	17,967	5,138	12,090	1,373
1997	384,465	410,821	198,815	99,463	39,908	35,561	18,737	4,246	12,587	1,502
1998	394,687	414,944	203,549	96,269	36,906	34,681	19,052	5,142	17,939	1,405
1999	408,405	421,379	213,619	96,576	35,718	29,848	19,058	5,831	19,291	1,439
2000	436,985	436,985	225,858	91,703	34,347	34,906	20,385	7,347	20,724	1,715

to receive assistance as households that do not include an elderly person—20% for each.

How much do all of these assistance programs cost us? There are several sources of assistance in the United States, although data are not collected for all programs. For example, data are collected on Aid to Families with Dependent Children (AFDC), Supplemental Security Income (SSI), and the General Assistance Program, but not for in-kind transfers, food stamps, or Medicaid. Total spending is summarized in Table 7.3 (numbers are in thousands of dollars).

One thing to keep in mind throughout all of this welfare consumption discussion is that only LPRs and refugees are eligible for public aid (with emergency medical care being the only obvious exception). Eligibility requirements were tightened in 1996 under the Illegal Immigration Reform and Responsibility Act. This law was designed to curb public assistance consumption by immigrants. Some of the eligibility restrictions are summarized in Table 7.4.

Table 7.4[6]

Current immigrant eligibility for welfare benefits

	SSI	Food stamps	Medicaid	TANF	Other federal means-tested benefits	State/local public benefits
Qualified immigrants arriving *before* **August 23, 1996**						
Legal permanent residents	Yes	No	State option	State option	State option	State option
Asylees, refugees[a]	Eligible for first 7 years	Eligible for first 5 years	Eligible for first 7 years	Eligible for first 5 years	Eligible for first 5 years	Eligible for first 5 years
Qualified immigrants arriving *after* **August 23, 1996**						
Legal permanent residents	No	No	Barred for first 5 years; then state option	Barred for first 5 years; then state option	Barred for first 5 years; then state option	State option
Asylees, refugees	Eligible for first 7 years	Eligible for first 5 years	Eligible for first 7 years	Eligible for first 5 years	Eligible for first 5 years	Eligible for first 5 years
Unqualified immigrants						
Illegal immigrants	No	No	Emergency services only	No	No[b]	No[c]
PRUCOL immigrants	No[d]	No	Emergency services only	No	No	No[c]

SSI = Suplemental Security Income
TANF = Temporary Assistance for Needy Families
PRUCOL = Persons residing under cover of law

a. This group includes Cuban and Haitian entrants, Amerasians, and granted withholding of deportation.
b. States have the option to provide WIC to unqualified immigrants.
c. Selected programs are exempted, including short-term noncash relief, immunizations, testing and treatment for communicable diseases, and selected assistance from community programs.
d. Those immigrants already receiving SSI as of August 22, 1996, continued to be eligible until September 30, 1998.

Source: Boeri, Hanson, and McCormick (2002).

There are several categories that are "state option." We already know that there are six immigrant states, but how do these six states compare in terms of generosity of public aid? Table 7.5 gives an interesting overview. All six of the immigrant states are at least as generous to immigrants as to natives, with most being more generous to immigrants. Illinois and Florida are generous only to immigrants, California is generous to everybody (but more generous to immigrants), New York and New Jersey are equally (very) generous to all, and Texas is not generous to anybody. So it seems that being an immigrant can never hurt in terms of states' generosity (well, for the six immigrant states at least). There are only seven states that are less generous to immigrants than they are to natives (those below the diagonal—Hawaii, Michigan, New Hampshire, Indiana, Oklahoma, South Carolina, and South Dakota).

---

[6] Hanson, "Why Does Immigration Divides America?" p. 15.

Chapter 7 | 145

Table 7.5

Availability of welfare benefits to immigrants by state, 1996–present

		Generosity of public assistance to all citizens			
		1	2	3	4
Public assistance availability to immigrants	4	Illinois	Missouri Nebraska	California Maine Maryland Massachusetts Rhode Island	Washington
	3	Florida	Oregon	Connecticut Minnesota New Jersey New York Pennsylvania Wisconsin	Hawaii
	2	Delaware District of Columbia Kentucky Montana Nevada North Carolina Tennessee Virginia Wyoming	Alaska Arizona Colorado Georgia Iowa Kansas New Mixico North Dakota Utah	Michigan	New Hampshire
	1	Alabama Arkansas Idaho Louisiana Mississippi Ohio Texas West Virginia	Indiana Oklahoma South Carolina South Dakota		

Note: Higher numbers indicate greater generosity of benefits to all citizens and greater availability of benefits to noncitizens.

Source: Zimmerman and Tumlin (1999).

What's the punch line for this chapter? First, it seems that immigrants are more prone to consume public aid than natives. It also seems that the propensity for immigrants to consume aid actually increases the longer the immigrant is here. Although I'm sure this is somewhat disturbing to many of you, remember that immigrants are really only a drop in the bucket as far as total numbers are concerned. There are simply far more natives on welfare and other assistance programs when you look at raw numbers. True, in percentage terms immigrants are more prone to consume, but if you ask "who drains the system more," you have to answer "natives do."

The graph in Figure 7.3 is an interesting way of summarizing the past few sections of this text. It was made via computer simulation that estimated the impact over time of a single immigrant.[7] The effect of this immigrant extends for 300 years! If you think this is ridiculous, just think of how Carnegie's or Rockefeller's economic impact continues to this day.

---

[7] James P. Smith and Barry Edmonston, eds., *The New Americans: Economic, Demographic, and Fiscal Effects of Immigration*, Washington, D.C.: National Academy Press, 1997, p. 341.

Figure 7.3

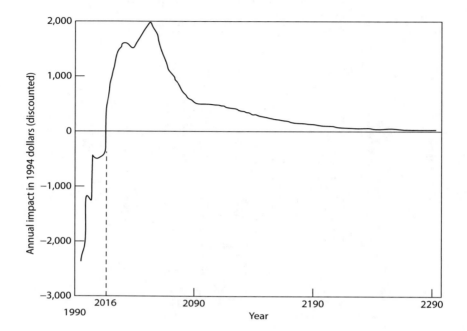

The immigrant arrives in about 1990, and at first has a negative impact thanks to their welfare consumption. However, this tapers over time, until 2016 when their impact becomes positive. This benefit then tapers off as time goes on. If you integrate the area beneath this curve to get the cumulative economic impact, you get something like an $80,000 net gain from a single immigrant. This is completely hypothetical of course, but it's a cool way to think of the long-term cost and benefit of immigration.

Chapter 8

Immigration Policy

Selling Liberty

We have talked at length about current United States immigration policy and how these policies have evolved over time. We have also seen many of the costs and benefits of immigration, and tried to justify either a pro-immigration or an anti-immigration opinion. This brings us to the last big topic: how should we decide who gets in and who doesn't? Some of the things that are hopefully rattling around in your head now include skills of immigrants, public good consumption, externalities, legal versus illegal immigration, enforcement costs, and so on. How do we piece all of this together to form policy recommendations for the big decision makers? Becoming an expert on immigration isn't worth much if you can't answer one simple question: "What should we do?"

This question strikes at the heart of economics since it is fundamentally a question of allocation. What is the best way to allocate admission to the United States? Currently, we use a fancy version of first-come, first-served, with some limits and exceptions. What does basic economic theory say about these types of allocation mechanisms? What is the best way to allocate something from an economic point of view? Price is the best way. It maximizes social welfare (go back and read Chapter 1 if you don't know what I'm talking about!). So why don't we use price to allocate admission? This would be simple to do—simply post a price for LPR status, and those who want to pay that price get it. We would have to adjust the price from time to time probably, based on demand or supply decisions we make, but the system would work very well (as all markets do). What are the issues with this? Well, it's not fair, for one thing. Poor people from poor countries couldn't afford to come here. Ok, so we can come up with a fancier formula for price that is somehow a function of per capita income in the country of origin. Then people from Sub-Saharan Africa would pay less than people from Western Europe. Fairness issue solved, right?

Interestingly, most people take issue with the idea of selling things like admission to the United States because those who cannot afford this good will suffer hardship. For this reason, we tend to impose price controls in markets where the good is deemed to have certain special properties like life-saving abilities (yes, immigration to the United

States probably saves many immigrants' lives—just think about medical facilities here versus elsewhere). For example, the market for kidney transplants has been tampered with in this way. We have imposed a price ceiling at a price of zero for organs—in the name of fairness. However, we can show via simple supply/demand diagram that this policy makes society worse off. Should we do this for LPR status as well? Will doing so make society worse off? Can we sell liberty?

In the other direction, should we set a price of zero for all goods that save lives? Is it wrong to sell medicine? We do in fact sell it, and it can save lives. We sell bread too, and tons of people starve to death. We sell vaccines and education and cars with airbags, too—all for a price greater than zero. So why not sell immigration?

Well, we kind of do already, actually. Recall that one of the criteria for obtaining admission is having $1 million to invest in a United States company. Also, we have imposed plenty of implicit costs (like paperwork) that people have to pay. But we can't bail out banks or pave roads with paperwork. We need cash. We have seen that about one million immigrants enter the country each year (or are adjusted to LPR status). If we charged each person, on average, $10,000 for becoming a permanent resident, that would raise 10 billion dollars a year. That's nearly equal to NASA's annual budget. (For the record, I think $10,000 is a bargain.)

Tradable Immigrant Certificates and Visas

If we are willing to accept the idea of explicitly selling the right to immigrate, then we can introduce and examine an entirely new possibility for the labor market involving immigrants—that of resalable visas. Suppose we sell, to companies in the United States, a bunch of visas that can be used to legally bring workers into the United States. If the labor demand of one company dwindles, or if the demand by other companies increases significantly, then the company may find it more profitable to sell the visa to another company. If we allow the resale of immigrant certificates in this way, we guarantee that the companies that want the immigrant workers the most get them. This is exactly our definition of efficiency. Thus, the resale of immigrant certificates increases surplus over the current system of first come, first served.

We would have to be careful in this scenario to define what rights to which possession of a certificate entitles a firm. For example, if a company fires an immigrant, do they retain the certificate to be reused later, or does the visa expire with the worker? (This is why I used both terms "visa" and "certificate" in the previous paragraph.) If the firm can keep and reuse the certificate, they may have an incentive to release their immigrant staff and resell their certificates to other firms in the event that a labor shortage increases the demand for immigrant labor (assuming the demand for immigrant labor increases at a faster rate than does the number of certificates).

This type of tradable certificate system has gained some fame recently thanks to the proposed tradable quota system for CO_2 emissions. It can be shown that most of the

Country of origin	Percent of group that fails the test
All countries	40.7
Europe	
France	7.4
Germany	14.4
Greece	30.6
Ireland	9.6
Italy	29.5
Portugal	70.1
United Kingdom	6.2
Americas	
Canada	12.2
Cuba	66.6
Dominican Republic	58.4
El Salvador	77.0
Haiti	54.1
Mexico	74.6
Nicaragua	56.6
Asia	
China	42.9
India	18.8
Korea	29.3
Vietnam	62.5
Philippines	15.0

Table 8.1[1]

problems with a tradable quota system can be addressed if the auction used for resale is designed properly and the number of certificates is reasonable. The result is in fact an increase in efficiency and social welfare. However, much like the CO_2 emissions case, these systems may be difficult to sell politically.

Canadian Point System

Canada has a sort of hybrid system for determining immigration eligibility. There is a series of questions you answer (it's a quiz, really), and based on your score, you are either eligible or not eligible for resident status in Canada. You can earn points for things like having an advanced degree or having money (price!) or migrating with somebody who has employment potential. (Speaking French gives you points.) An unofficial version of this quiz can be found at <http://www.workpermit.com/canada/points_calculator.htm>. (Seriously, I cannot confirm the security for this webpage, so use with caution.) One major underlying theme of the Canadian quiz is that people with more skills are admitted preferably over those with less skill.

---

[1] Borjas, *Heaven's Door*, p. 196.

Table 8.2[2]

The Immigration Surplus and Immigration Policy (immigration surplus in billions of dollars)

	Policy option		
	All immigrants are unskilled	30 percent of immigrants are skilled	All immigrants are skilled
Short-run: The capital stock is fixed			
Wage of native workers is not very responsive to immigration	8.4	6.8	42.0
Wage of native workers is very responsive to immigration	22.4	21.2	126.0
Long-run: The capital stock adjusts to immigration			
Wage of native workers is not very responsive to immigration	8.0	1.9	8.0
Wage of native workers is very responsive to immigration	20.0	3.9	20.0

How would the United States fare if it adopted a similar policy? Would the demographics here be that much different from what they are today? Take a look at Table 8.2, which explores this possibility. Under a hypothetical point system for the United States, this gives the percent of immigrants by location of origin that would fail the test. The hypothetical point system gives 50 points for a high school diploma, 25 points if under the age of forty (a good working age), and 25 points if fluent in English. Passing is 75 or higher.

Do you see the percent of immigrants from Mexico that would fail—75%! Needless to say, the demographics of the United States would be vastly different under this system. A 75% reduction amounts to about 10 million fewer Mexican immigrants.

Did the United States make a mistake in abandoning the skill-based policies of the pre-1965 era? The following table revisits the idea of immigration surplus under a couple of hypothetical immigration policies concerning skill.

Similar to the point system used in Canada is that of Australia and New Zealand. All of these systems are designed to select immigrants based on a couple of broad categories: humanitarian (e.g., refugees), social (e.g., family reunification), and economic (e.g., jobs). The details of the criteria (i.e., the "correct" answers to the quiz) can then be tailored to achieve the desired number of immigrants from each category. Below is

---

[2] Borjas, *Heaven's Door*, p. 102.

a summary of recent targets and actual levels of immigration for these point-system countries.[3]

Table 8.3

Canada* Immigration Category					
		humanitarian objectives (% of total)	social objectives (% of total)	economic objectives (% of total)	Total Immigration
2004	planning levels	28,100-32,500 14%	59,000-64,500 28%	132,000-147,000 60%	220,000-245,000
	actual immigration	25,984 12%	65,124 29%	121,050 55%	221,355
2005	planning levels	29,400-32,800 14%	52,500-55,500 24%	132,000-148,000 62%	220,000-245,000
	actual immigration	32,686 14%	62,246 26%	133,746 57%	235,824
Australia Immigration Category					
		humanitarian objectives (% of total)	social objectives (% of total)	economic objectives (% of total)	Total Immigration
2004	planning levels	12,000 n.a.	40,600 39%	63,300 60%	100,000-110,000
	actual immigration	13,851 11%	42,230 33%	71,240 56%	127,321
2005	planning levels	13,000 n.a.	42,000 36%	72,100 65%	105,000-115,000
	actual immigration	13,178 10%	41,740 31%	77,880 59%	132,798
New Zealand Immigration Category					
		humanitarian objectives (% of total)	social objectives (% of total)	economic objectives (% of total)	Total Immigration
2004	planning levels	4,500 10%	13,500 30%	27,000 60%	45,000
	actual immigration	4,959 13%	13,462 35%	20,596 53%	39,017
2005	planning levels	4,500 10%	13,500 30%	27,000 60%	45,000
	actual immigration	5,040 10%	13,949 29%	29,826 61%	48,815

---

[3] Zimmermann, Klaus, H. Bonin, R. Fahr, and H. Hinte. "Immigration Policy and the Labor Market: The German Experience and Lessons for Europe." Springer (2007).

Although the criteria and quiz scoring varies slightly by location (see table below), the thrust is the same: if you are a certain age, have a certain wealth, and have certain skills, then you will score high enough to enter these countries.

One problem with the point system, however, is that it may be slow to respond to changing demand for immigrant labor. For example, short-term periods of excessive growth or recession will affect the demand for workers, and in the absence of a more salient market system (yay price!), the market for immigrant labor may not clear.

The points systems of New Zealand, Australia and Canada

New Zealand	Australia	Canada
A. labor market factors		
1. educational attainment / skills		
55 points for recognised post-graduate qualification (Masters degree, doctorate)	**60 points** for most occupations where training is specific to the occupation	**25 points** for PhD or Masters degree and at least 17 years of full-time or full-time equivalent study
50 points for recognised basic qualification (e.g. trade qualification, diploma, bachelors degree, bachelors degree with Honours)	**50 points** for more general professional occupations	**22 points** for two or more university degrees at the Bachelor's level or a three-year diploma, trade certificate or apprenticeship and at least 15 years of full-time or full-time equivalent study
10 bonus points for qualification in an area of absolute skills shortage	**40 points** for other general skilled occupations	**20 points** for a two-year university degree at the Bachelor's level or a two-year diploma, trade certificate or apprenticeship and at least 14 years of full-time or full-time equivalent study.
5 bonus points for qualification in an identified future growth area or cluster		**15 points** for a one-year diploma, trade certificate Bachelor's level or a one-year diploma, trade certificate or apprenticeship and at least 13 years of full-time or full-time equivalent study
		12 points for a one-year diploma, trade certificate or apprenticeship and at least 12 years of full-time or full-time equivalent study
		5 points for secondary school educational credentials
2. qualification acquired within the host country		
10 bonus points for recognised New Zealand qualification (and at least two years study in NZ)	**15 points** for completion of an Australian doctorate at an Australian educational institution after a period of at least 2 years full-time while in Australia	*5 bonus points,* if applicant or spouse have completed a post-secondary program of at least two years in Canada since the age of 17[2])
	10 points for completion of an Australian Master of Honours degree (at least upper second class level) at an Australian educational institution while in Australia after having completed an Australian bachelor degree as a result of at least 1 year full-time study while in Australia	
	5 points for completion of a full-time study in Australia for a total of at least 2 years towards the award degree, diploma or trade qualification	
	5 points for having lived and studied for at least 2 years in one or more areas in regional Australia or low population growth metropolitan areas	
3. work experience		
Points for work experience: **10 points** for 2 years **15 points** for 4 years **20 points** for 6 years **25 points** for 8 years **30 points** for 10 years Bonus points for work experience in New Zealand:	**10 points,** if the nominated occupation is worth 60 points under skills, and the applicant has worked in his/her nominated occupation, or a closely related occupation, for at least 3 out of the 4 years immediately before his/her application **5 points,** if the nominated occupation is worth 40. 50 or 60 points under skills, and the applicant has worked in any occupation on the Skilled	Applicant must have at least one year of full-time experience in the last 10 years in a management or professional or highly skilled occupation as listed on the National Occupational Classification (NOC) as Skill Type O, A or B. If applicant's occupation does not come under one of these skill levels or his/her experience did not occur in the last 10 years, his/her application will be refused

5 points for 2 years
10 points for 4 years
15 points for 6 years or more

Additional *bonus points* for work experience in an identified future growth area or cluster
5 points for 2 to 5 years
10 points for 6 years or more

Additional *bonus points* for work experience in an area of absolute skills shortage:
10 points for 2 to 5 years
15 points for 6 years or more

Occupations List (SOL) for at least 3 out of the 4 years immediately before before his/her application

5 bonus points for at least 6 months' worth of Austrialian work experience in the 4 years before lodging an application in an occupation on the SOL[1])

Points vary in years of experience:
15 points for 1 year
17 points for 2 years
19 points for 3 years
21 points for 4 or more years

5 bonus points if applicant or spouse has been working full-time in Canada for at least one year[2])

4. job opportunities / sponsoring of predefined occupational groups

60 points for current skilled employment in New Zwealand for 12 months or more

50 points for an offer of skilled employment in New Zealand or a current skilled employment in New Zealand for less than 12 months

Bonus points for employment or offer of employment:
5 points for an identified future growth area or cluster
10 points for an area of absolute skills shortage
10 points for a region outside Auckland

20 points if applicant's nominated occupation is listed on the Migration Occupations in Demand List (MODL) - in connection with job offer

15 points if applicant's nominated occupation is listed on the MODL, but no job offer

10 points if applicant has a permanent offer of employment approved by Human Resources and Skills Development Canada (HRSDC)

Applicant is in Canada, holding a temporary work permit:

10 points if employment is validated by HRSDC, including sectoral confirmations

10 points if employment is exempt from HRSDC validation under international agreements (e.g. NAFTA) or significantly benefits Canada (i.e. intra-company transfereee)

5 bonus points if applicant receives points in one of these three cases [2)]

5. alternative requirements investor / business category

Immediate application for permanent residence is only possible under the *Investor* category.
Applicants must:
- be under 55 years of age
- meet health and character requirements (B.2.)
- meet language requirements (B.1.)
- have at least 5 years' business experience
- have NZD 2,000,000 (€ 1,138,000) to invest for five years
Invested funds will be held by the NZ government for five years and be adjusted for inflation during this time. Funds cannot be invested in any other way. After two years half of that money may be withdrawn to be invested in a business that will benefit NZ. Submitting a business plan is mandatory for this end.

Applying under the *Entrepreneur* category is only possible if applicant held a Long Term Business Visa / Permit before. Applicants must have successfully established a business in NZ that is benefiting NZ. To be eligible regulations under (B.1.) and (B.2.) apply. Applicants must not have applied for or been granted social welfare benefits in NZ.

Immediate application for permanent residence is only possible under the *Business Talent (Migrant)* category. All applicants in the *Business Owner I Senior Executive I Investor* categories will have to apply for a provisional visa valid for four years before they can apply for permanent residence. Applicants under these categories may have sponsorship by a State/Territory government. Those will be considered against lower threshold criteria. Applicants must generally be under 45 years of age and have business and private assets of a min. net value of AUD 500,000 [AUD 250,000] (€314,000 [€157,000]) at their disposal (*Business Owner* and *Senior Executive* categories). AUD 2,250,000 [AUD 1,125,000] (€ 1,413,000 [€ 706,500]) worth of assets are required for the *Investor* category.

Business Talent (Migrant):
- need of State/Territory sponsorship
- applicant under 55 years of age or proposing to establish or participate in a business that was determined to be of exceptional economic benefit to State/Territory

- business and personal assets of a min. net value of AUD 1,500,000 (€ 942,000).

Individual appropriateness criteria (B.2.) apply. If unsponsored, applicants must have vocational English.

Immigration is possible for eighter *investors, entrepreneurs* or *self-employed persons.*

Investors:
- must have a net worth of CAD 800,000 (€ 565,000)
- must make an investment of CAD 400,000 (€ 282,500). payable to the Receiver General of Canada (investments are allocated to provinces and used for job creation / economic development
- full amount of investment is repaid (without interest) to the investor after five years
- are not required to start a business
- no immigration conditions are imposed

Entrepreneurs:
- must have a net worth of CAD 300,000 (€ 212,000)
- must control at least 1/3 of equity of and provided management to a qualifying Canadian business
- must create at least 1 full-time job equivalent for one or more Canadian citizens / residents

Self-employed persons:
must have the experience, ability and intention to either:
- establilish a business that will create at least employment for themselves and make a significant contribution to cultural activities or athletics in Canada, *or*
- purchase and manage a farm

Applicants under all three categories must score 35 out of a possible 100 in a points test. Criteria are:
- Business experience (20 to 35 points / 2 to 5 years)
- Age (A.6.)
- Education (A.1.)
Language proficiency (B.1.)

- Adaptability:
6 points for a business exploration trip CDN in the five years prior to application
6 points for participation in joint federal-provincial business immigration initiatives

Individual appropriateness criteria apply (*B.2.*).

6. age

30 points for age from 20 to 29	**30 points** for age from 18 to 29	**10 points** for age from 21 to 49
25 points for age from 30 to 39	**25 points** for age from 30 to 34	**8 points** for age 20 and 50
20 points for age from 40 to 44	**20 points** for age from 35 to 39	**6 points** for age 19 and 51
10 points for age from 45 to 49	**15 points** for age from 40 to 44	**4 points** for age 18 and 52
5 points for age from 50 to 55		**2 points** for age 17 and 53
Applicant must be < 56 years of age	Applicant must be < 45 years of age	No points awarded <17 and > 53 years of age

Notes: 1) Even if all three bonus criteria are men, only 5 bonus points may be awarded.
2) Up to 10 bonus points on any combination of the according elements.

B. integration factors

1. language proficiency

no points, but a minimum standard of English is required (amoungst others, IELTS certificate, recognised qualifications taught entirely in English and working in skilled employment in New Zealand are accepted as a verification)

20 points for competent English (a generally effective command of the language, and the ability to use and understand fairly complex language, particularly in familiar situations)

15 points for Vocational English (a reasonable command of the English language, coping with overall meaning in most situations and the ability to communicate effectively in nominated field of employment)

5 bonus points for fluency in one of Australia's community languages (other than English) [1]

Up to 24 points for high proficiency in English and French

Up to 16 points for fluency in one of these languages and no proficiency in the other one

4 to 8 points for basic proficiency in both languages

2. individual appropriateness

All persons included in an application must meet health requirements

All persons included in an application must be of good character. Applicants aged ≥ 17 must provide police certificates for their country of citizenship and for every country in which they have lived for 12 months or more (whether on one visit or intermittently) in the 10 years before the date they lodge their application.

Applicants are asked to undertake an examination by a physician selected by Australian authorities. Costs incurred must be covered by applicants.

To enter Australia, applicants must be of good character. Applicants may be asked to provide police certificates of each country they resided in for 12 months or more in the last 10 years. Applicants may be required to provide personal details to facilitate additional character checks.

Applicants must pass a medical examination before coming to Canada. Application for permanent residence will not be accepted if that person's health:
- is a danger to public health or safety;
- or would cause excessive demand on health or social services in Canada.

Applicants must provide police certificates for all countries they have resided in for 6 months or more since reaching the age of 18.

3. relations in the host country

10 points for close family in New Zealand

15 points for close family in Australia

5 points for applicant's or spouse's close family in Canada [2]

4. assets

Principal applicants with dependent children must show that they meet a min. income requirement if they come to New Zealand, which is to ensure they can support themselves and dependents. Minimum family income requirements are: NZD 30,946 (€ 17,639) / 1 child, NZD 36,493 (€ 20,801) / 2 children, NZD 42,040 (€ 32,962) / 3 children, NZD 47,568 (€ 27,114) / 4 or more children. Spouse's/partner's income may be taken into account.

5 bonus points for capital investment in Australia [minimum of AUD 100,000 (€ 60,100)] [1]

Minimum funds required depending on size of family unit:
CAD 9,897 (€ 6,698) / 1 person,
CAD 12,372 (€ 8,377) / 2 persons,
CAD 15,387 (€ 10,419) / 3 persons,
CAD 18,626 (€ 12,612) / 4 persons,
CAD 20,821 (€ 14,098) / 5 persons,
CAD 23,015 (€ 15,583) / 6 persons,
CAD 25,210 (€ 17,069) / 7 or more persons.

5. spouse's qualification

10 bonus points for spouse's/partner's qualifications

10 bonus points for spouse's/partner's employment or offer of employment

5 points, if applicant's spouse is able to satisfy basic requirements of age, English language ability, qualifications, nominated occupation and recent work experience and has obtained a suitable skills assessment from the relevant assessing authority for his/her nominated occupation

3 points *for completion of a one or two-year post-secondary program and at least 13 years of education*

4 points *for completion of a three-year post-secondary program of a three-year university degree and at leoast 15 years of education*

5 points *for completion of a Master's or Ph.D. and at least 17 years of education* [2]

C. minimum score		
100 points	110/120 points	67 points

D. fees		
Depending on country of citizenship, current location and Visa/Permit type; e.g., fees for European and most other countries of citizenship or current locations amount to: NZD 290 (€ 165) for Work Visa Talent and Work Visa Long Term Skill Shortages List, NZD 200 (€ 114) for Work Visa other, NZD 1360 (€ 773) for Residence - skilled migrants category, NZD 2200 (€ 1250) for Residence - Business Investor/Entrepreneur, NZD 1200 (€ 682) for Residence - other	Visa application charges have to be paid in two installments. The 1st installment is usually paid on lodging an application for the application to be valid. Depending on what class of migration is chosen, costs for the 1st installment may range from AUD 1,305 (€855) (Employer Sponsored Migration) to AUD 3,760 (€ 2,455) (Business Talent [Migrant]). The 2nd installment is not required in every case. AUD 1,885 (€ 1,230) for Skill Matching (General Skilled Migration, primary applicant only), AUD 2,690 (€ 1,755) for any secondary applicant over 18 with less than functional English, AUD 5,395 (€ 3,520) for a primary applicant with less than functional English (Employer Sponsored Migration and some types of Business Skills Migration only)	*Investor, Entrepreneur or Self-employed Persons Class applicants:* principal applicant: CAD 1,050 (€ 711) *Other classes of applicants:* principal applicant: CAD 550 (€ 372) *All classes:* family member of principal applicant 22 years of age or older, or less than 22 years of age being spouse or common-law partner: CAD 550 (€ 372) family member of principal applicant less than 22 years of age not being spouse or common-law partner: CAD 150 (€ 102) *Right of Permanent Residence Fee:* CAD 975 (€ 661). payable for principal applicant and spouse or common-law partner *Work permit:* CAD 150 (€ 102)

Sources: NZ (1/2): http://www.immigration.govt.nz/migrant/popups/pointstable.htm; NZ (2/2): http://www.immigration.govt.nz/migrant/popups/bonuspointstable.htm; AUS: http://www.immi.gov.au/allforms/booklets/1119.pdf; CDN: http://www.cic.gc.ca/english/skilled/qual-5.html.

Illegal Immigration as Immigration Policy

I want you to realize that the problem of a shortage of immigrant labor is not unique to point systems. The United States also faces this issue since we too use an allocation mechanism that is not price (remember, we use first come, first served). But, the United States has a secret weapon—illegal immigration! It is in fact illegal immigration that clears the market for immigrant labor in the United States, as we have seen earlier. This is why as the economy booms, so does the number of illegal immigrants. As such, a good immigration policy may include, at lease implicitly, allowance for illegal immigration.

Let's extend this reasoning to the limiting case, where our immigration policy is as follows: immigration is not allowed. If you are from another country, then you are here illegally. Obviously, this policy wouldn't have worked historically, since the vast majority (and I mean vast) of Americans are from elsewhere, or are at least descendants of people who came from elsewhere. (I wonder if my use of the term "native" Americans has been problematic for people who are actually Native Americans.) However, this is a policy that we can implement now. So we would say, "from now on, no immigrants."[4]

What would happen to immigrant population? Would we actually see no new immigrants crossing our borders? No. We currently see people migrating illegally, so why would a strengthening of the law change this? If we strengthened the penalty, we might see a reduction of immigration ("all immigrants will be shot on sight!" is not a good campaign platform…), but even then I would guess that some people would

---

[4] Our choice of cuisines would certainly not be good if we had implemented this policy from day one. There would be no pizza, no German beer, and no sushi!

view the benefits of migrating to outweigh the risk. So let's agree that outlawing all immigration would not eliminate immigration. However, this policy would certainly change the mix of immigrants. No longer would you see foreign exchange students, for example—I would not believe that the risk of being caught would be outweighed by the benefit of a diploma. This should be no surprise, since we have seen several cases of how policy changes can affect the demographic mix of immigrants.

Can we make any claims about the cost of enforcing this policy? We could fire anybody who currently works in the Citizenship and Immigration Office (part of the Department of Homeland Security), since their services would no longer be needed. However, we would probably need to add personnel to the other branches of the Department of Homeland Security that are responsible for border protection (Coast Guard, Bureau of Customs and Border Protection, et cetera). This might be costly, especially in light of the fact that our culture in the United States is so diverse and heterogeneous. Identifying new immigrants would be very difficult with all of these existing immigrants and their descendants running around. How would you handle international flights at airports? Could you guarantee that visitors leave? What if they come for a week's vacation and never return? (Remember, overstaying a visa accounts for nearly half of our current illegal immigrants.) For all of these reasons, I anticipate the cost of enforcing the policy would be enormous.

But who says we need to catch everybody? Even better, who says we need to catch anybody? Might it be possible for us to pick a penalty for illegal immigration that is sufficiently strict such that potential immigrants decide that the risk of getting caught outweighs the benefit of migrating?[5] The penalty would have to be large, and most importantly, it would have to be credible. I'm sure you've all experienced this with your parents—your mother threatens that if you stay out too late, you'll be in big trouble, but then when you get caught you put on your best sad face and she lets you off the hook. (My dog is really good at this. I actually believe she regrets jumping on the table and eating my steak.) If the threat is credible, if it is believable, then we may be able to "enforce" a policy that actually limits the amount of immigration without ever actually lifting a finger. However, any lack of credibility undermines the policy—and most governments have a problem seeming credible. This is a game theory result—in repeated games, if you ever violate the trust of the other party, they may never trust you again. This is clarified in the next chapter.

For now, we close with one last article concerning the future of immigration enforcement.

---

[5] To give you the punch line before I finish the setup, the answer is "yes." Although the math is beyond the reach of most undergraduates, a proof can be found in Bernotas, David, D. Glycopantis, and N. Yannelis, "Extensive Form Implementation of Weak Fine Core Allocations Through Penalties," *Essays in Economic Theory, Growth and Labor Markets*, Bitros and Katsoulacos eds. (2002)

Deportation Program Grows

Texas Fully Adopts Much-Debated Federal Plan Aimed at All Counties by 2013

By Ana Campoy

Wall Street Journal, October 18, 2010

Austin, Texas—A federal program that scans local jails for illegal immigrants is being expanded across the state, the latest front in the nation's battle over immigration policy.

In the past two weeks, Texas became the first border state to fully deploy the department of Homeland Security program, which is scheduled to be rolled out to all U.S. counties by 2013. The program automatically routes prisoners' fingerprints to the department, which tries to determine whether they are allowed to be in the U.S.

Known as Secure Communities, the program is designed to intercept and remove illegal immigrants who have been convicted of serious crimes such as homicide, rape and kidnapping, immigration officials say.

But immigrant groups and lawyers argue it is singling out immigrants with no serious criminal record, clogging up the courts. Political analysts say Secure Communities and related programs are alienating Democratic-leaning Hispanic voters from the Obama administration.

"Why are we wasting funds to deport people who aren't even supposed to be targets of the program?" said Jim Harrington, director of the Texas Civil Rights Projects, which provides legal assistance to low-income people.

Proponents of stricter immigration controls contend Secure Communities is a step in the right direction to protect the nation from dangerous illegal immigrants.

"Every day, we have murders and serious crimes committed against citizens and legal immigrants," said Janice Kephart, national-security policy director at the Center for Immigration Studies, which favors curbing all immigration to the U.S. "It is a public-safety issue."

The expanded program comes at a time when a national debate is raging over Arizona's immigration law, which would require local police to check the immigration status of people stopped for other possible violations.

The federal government has successfully blocked that law in court so far, arguing it shifts responsibility for immigration enforcement from federal to local officials.

Unlike the Arizona law, Secure Communities doesn't require local law enforcement to perform any additional tasks. Using fingerprints the police already have collected for the Federal Bureau of Investigation, it merges those records with Homeland Security's database, which contains all legal and some illegal entrants into the U.S. That assists the department in identifying criminal suspects in violation of immigration laws. If the fingerprints don't match any record, Homeland Security can deploy immigration officers to the jail to investigate further.

Last week, Homeland Security Secretary Janet Napolitano touted the success of the program, saying Secure Communities contributed to a 70% increase since 2008 in deportations of criminal suspects who were illegal immigrants.

But many in the Hispanic community are frustrated over Secure Communities and related Obama administration programs, which they see as a step-up in deportations without addressing other facets of the immigration debate, such as whether there will be a path to citizenship for illegal immigrants.

"Not only are they not helping to solve the issue, but they are criminalizing more immigrants," said union organizer Ben Monterroso of Secure Communities.

As head of a multistate campaign to boost Latino turnout, he is trying to persuade Latinos to put their frustration aside and go to the polls. A recent poll by the Pew Hispanic Center shows that Latinos are less motivated than other voters to go to the polls in November.

In Arlington, Va., and Santa Clara County, Calif., local officials recently passed resolutions to opt out from Secure Communities in response to community concerns that the program would make immigrants afraid of the police and result in the deportation of non-criminals.

Since 2008, when Secure Communities debuted in individual counties around the nation, more than a quarter of the illegal immigrants identified by the program and sent back to their countries of origin were non-criminals, government statistics show.

In Travis County, Texas, where Austin sits, about 1,000 immigrants have been removed since the program was deployed in the county in 2009. More than 30% had no criminal record.

In San Antonio, the nearest immigration court, the number of pending cases has grown to about 4,800 so far this year, compared with 1,821 in 2008, according to data compiled by the Transactional Records Access Clearinghouse at Syracuse University.

Noe Jimenez Ruano, a day laborer from Guatemala, was arrested for criminal trespassing in July while standing outside an Austin business looking for work, according to his lawyer and the director of the shelter where he lived.

A magistrate judge found no probable cause for the arrest, but immigration officials learned he was in the country illegally through the booking process and deported him last month.

Nicole True, Mr. Jimenez Ruano's lawyer, said, "People forget that the way someone ends up in jail is based on a human being making a decision."

Homeland Security has said that while Secure Communities focuses on dangerous criminals, the agency has the authority to remove anyone who enters the U.S. illegally.

An agency official said some immigrants categorized as non-criminal have lengthy rap sheets of charges and arrests but have never been convicted.

Chapter 9

Game Theory and Immigration Policy

Overview of Game Theory[1]

Games have obviously been around since soon after the beginning of time. Game theory isn't quite that old, but it emerged with rigor in economics after the publication of a book in 1944 by John von Neumann and Oskar Morgenstern called *Theory of Games and Economic Behavior*. Unlike most things in economics and academics, the name "game theory" is actually not misleading at all—it is simply the study of how we play games. For example, von Neumann and Morgenstern begin by examining card games and other games of chance. From there, we can introduce games that involve interaction between multiple parties over multiple periods. By developing an understanding of how people behave in these situations, we can enrich our understanding of how people—both firms and consumers—interact with each other in our economic framework. This is the broad goal of game theory—to model and understand how people interact.

A game is made up of several necessary components:
1. a list of players;
2. available actions for each player;
3. a description of the information available to each player;
4. a relationship between actions and payoffs;
5. preferences or goals for each player.

Interestingly, there are a couple of different ways to incorporate these components into a diagram of a game. One way is to use a game tree, called an extensive form, to show the moves and outcomes of the game. Extensive form games work in the same

---

[1] I will limit this section to a superficial treatment of only the most relevant topics in game theory. For a more complete (and in my opinion, wonderfully readable) treatment, I direct you to Joel Watson's *Strategy* text. I have in fact stolen much of the content in this section directly from this text. For those of you with a game theory background, don't let the sloppy treatment here frustrate you. The conclusions are valid despite my lack of rigor.

part of your brain as flow chart diagrams—nodes connected with arrows that direct you either this way or that way. These are particularly useful for games that involve taking turns by participants (first you move, then it's my turn). For simultaneous games (rock, paper, scissors), the best way to write out the game is to use the *normal form* representation. This is a matrix where the columns are assigned to one player, and the rows are assigned to the other.

Here is an example of a very simple game and its normal form representation. The game is called "matching pennies." Player 1and Player 2 each have a penny (let's call them P1 and P2). Each player will flip their coin in private (so that their opponent cannot see the outcome of the coin toss). Then, the players will simultaneously announce either heads or tails. (Notice that I did not say "each player will announce the outcome of the coin toss." That is because players can lie, and announce "heads" even if the coin toss was tails.) If the announcements match (heads-heads, or tails-tails) then P2 must give his penny to P1. (Remember, both players announce at exactly the same time.) If the announcements do not match (heads-tails or tails-heads) then P1 must give his penny to P2. The payoffs are thus either +1 cent if you win or -1 cent if you lose.

Keep in mind, I have to clearly specify all 5 things listed above:
1. Players: P1and P2
2. Actions: announce either heads (H) or tails (T)
3. Information: I know only the result of my coin toss; I don't see your coin. Same goes for you.
4. The relationship between actions and payoffs: if the announcements match (HH or TT), then P1 wins P2's penny. If they don't match (HT or TH), then P2 wins P1's penny.
5. Preferences: to win as much money as possible.

Below is the normal form matrix for this game. P1 is on left, so each row represents a possible move for P1. P2 is on the top, so each column is a move for P2. The ordered pairs of payoffs are written with P1's payoff first, then P2's. (That is, the ordered pair (-1,1) means P1 loses one cent, P2 wins one cent.)

	P2 H	P2 T
P1 H	(1, -1)	(-1, 1)
P1 T	(-1, 1)	(1, -1)

Verify that this matrix displays all of the information of #1 to #5. Also please note how easy it is to read this table—if P1 moves H and P2 moves T, then P1 gets -1 and

P2 gets 1. Any thoughts on how you would play this game? What's your best strategy for announcing heads or tails? Will you ever lie, always lie, or never lie?[2]

Below is another game that you may have seen before. This is called the "prisoners' dilemma." The story goes something like this: two people are captured on suspicion that they committed a crime. The suspects are separated into different rooms so that they cannot hear or see the other person, and they are interrogated. Each is told that if they rat out their partner, they will receive a lighter sentence in exchange for their confession. However, there is not enough evidence to convict them both without a confession from at least one of them, so if they both keep quiet about the crime, then the police will be forced to let them go with only a small fine. However, the worst case for either person would be to remain quiet while the other guy rats, since then you are found guilty without the benefit of a reduced sentence for confessing. Here are the 5 components for this game:

1. The players here are still P1 and P2
2. Actions: each player can be quiet (Q) or rat (R)
3. Information: just like the matching pennies game, I will have no information about what you do until I am informed of the payoffs.
4. Payoffs: if we both rat, we are both in trouble, but we do both get leniency because of our confessions. Thus, the payoff for that cell will be small, but not zero. If we are both quiet, we do better, so the payoff here will be slightly larger than if we both rat. If you rat and I stay quiet, I'm screwed. I go to jail for a long time and you go free. Your payoff here will be huge; mine will be tiny (zero).
5. Preferences: to maximize our payoff (minimize time in jail).

The normal form for this prisoners' dilemma is below.

		P2	
		Q	R
P1	Q	(2, 2)	(0, 3)
	R	(3, 0)	(1, 1)

Take a second to double check that this makes sense. If P1 plays R (the bottom row) and P2 plays Q (the left column), the payoff is (3,0), which means P1 gets 3 (he's

---

[2] Finding the solution requires tools that we don't need here, but I can tell you that it is optimal for you to always tell the truth in this game, assuming you both have fair coins. If you played this game over and over again, you would expect to earn exactly zero cents—you would win just as often as you would lose. That's the best you can do.

happy) and P2 gets 0 (he's screwed). This makes sense given the story. Keep in mind that these numbers are payoffs—do not interpret them as time in jail (you would need to put minus signs in from of them if you want this interpretation).

How would you play this game? You might have the instinct to say "I want 3, since it's the highest payoff," which is true. In order to get 3, you have to play R—you have rat. So, you think "I'm going to rat no matter what the other guy does," but since the rules apply to him too, he's thinking the same exact thing. This means that he's going to rat, and you already decided to rat, so you end up both playing move R, and you get (1,1) as your payoff.

That might not seem that bad at first, but notice that there is a way for you guys to both double your payoffs to (2,2) if you would instead both keep quiet. So why don't you instead play Q instead of R? Well, you're no dummy, and you realize that playing Q in an attempt to get the payoff of 2 leaves you open to get screwed by the other guy—if you play Q and he plays R, you get zero! (This is the top, right cell if you are P1.) The risk is too great. You prefer to settle for 1 (by playing R) than risk getting 0 (by playing Q).

So how can we figure out a way to end up at (2,2), making both of us better off without leaving either of us open to the risk of getting screwed? We need to cooperate. Maybe we could come to an agreement to keep quiet (I'm sure many criminals have entered a similar agreement with their accomplices). Unfortunately, if the game is a one-shot deal, this won't happen. I have nothing to lose by screwing you over and ratting, since the game is only one shot. If I rat, you have no way of getting even with me. However, if the game is repeated (meaning we play it over and over), then such an agreement can work. The reason is simple: if I screw you in round 1 by playing R when you played Q, then you can switch to R in round 2 and protect yourself from future damage.[3] In this way, repeating the game may influence how you play, and in turn what the equilibrium payoffs are.

Cooperative Equilibria

When can we reach a cooperative equilibrium in a game? In other words, when can we form an agreement that both of us will voluntarily adhere to? Intuitively, I will adhere to our agreement if doing so gives me a higher long-run payoff than cheating does. The key is to think *long-run* payoff, not immediate payoff. Cheating will improve your payoff today, but eventually, the revenge from the other player may outweigh that

---

[3] I know you're probably thinking "yeah, but switching to R after the damage is done doesn't really help me get even," which a true statement. The damage is done. However, it is possible for us to change the payoffs or complicate the game in such a way that this retribution does even the score. We're keeping it simple here, so we lose a bit of realism.

one-time gain. To see this, let's revisit the prisoners' dilemma game discussed in the previous section.

We saw in the section on present value in Chapter 3 that we can do some calculations involving the interest rate to capture your feelings and expectations about the future, which in turn affected your migration decision today. A similar method can be used to show how the impact of future rounds of the game influence your decision on what move to play in round 1. Let's use the Greek letter delta to represent the discount factor or discount rate. [4] (I am intentionally using a different letter so as to not confuse this material with the PV calculations done earlier. You'll see why in a second.) If both people always played Q in the prisoners' dilemma game, the payoff to both would be 2 in each round. However, just as we saw earlier, a payoff of 2 today and a payoff of 2 tomorrow have different value in today's dollars. Specifically, a payoff of 2 today is worth only 2δ tomorrow for some δ between 0 and 1.

Right now you're thinking "You messed up! 2 today should be worth *more* than 2 tomorrow—and 2δ is less than 2." I didn't screw up—I promise. Here's why. If I offer to give you $2 today, or instead you could wait and get $2 tomorrow, which is a better deal? Clearly $2 today is better—why wait until tomorrow? More technically speaking, you would prefer the $2 today because you could then use the $2 to earn interest, *et cetera*, so that by the time tomorrow arrives, you have more than $2. It would actually be worth $2(1+r)$, where r is our old friend the interest rate. And now you say "Aha! I knew you screwed up! $2 today is worth something like $2.10 by the time tomorrow arrives." Yes, but asking "$2 is equivalent to how much come tomorrow?" is not the same as asking "$2 tomorrow is worth how much today?" These two questions are sort of opposites. In fact, you can easily show that the discount rate δ is equal to $\frac{1}{1+r}$ which we used earlier. Remember, $\delta \neq r$. The best way to think about the discount rate δ is this: δ tells me how much you value tomorrow compared to today. Thus, as δ gets close to 1, to you, tomorrow will become just as important as today. If δ falls, tomorrow becomes less important to you. (Big δ means you eat healthy food, small δ means you eat lots of junk food.)

So, back to the long-term payoffs for the repeated game when both people always play Q, resulting in a payoff of 2 each period. Over several rounds, including the discount factor, the long-term payoff for this strategy would be

$$2 + 2\delta + 2\delta^2 + 2\delta^3 + \ldots$$

If we assume that the number of periods is large, this (infinite) sum becomes something nice:

$$2 + 2\delta + 2\delta^2 + 2\delta^3 + \ldots = \frac{2}{1 + \delta}.$$

---

[4] See Watson, p. 265.

The derivation of this follows the procedure used in Chapter 3.

So the payoff for following the agreement and always playing Q is $\frac{2}{1+\delta}$. What is the payoff for cheating? Don't say 3—because that's the short-run payoff of cheating only. You have to also factor in the payoffs for every period after you cheat, and if you recall the story we told, once you cheat, the other guy is going to play R forever, giving you a payoff of 1 each period for the rest of your life. Thus, if you cheat, you get 3 today, and 1 for the rest of eternity. The sum of payoffs then looks like this:

$$3 + 1\delta + 1\delta^2 + 1\delta^3 + \ldots = 3 + \frac{1}{1+\delta}.$$

Something that might not be obvious at first glance is the fact that it doesn't matter when you decide to cheat. You could play 576 rounds of the game, following the agreement to play Q the entire time, and then randomly cheat and play R in round 577. From that point on, your payoff is given by the formula above. Same is true if you consider violating the agreement in round 1 instead of round 577—you're concerned only with how cheating affects your *future* payoffs. What's done is done, so you ignore the past when making the decision to cheat or play fair. Thus, the calculation you make in your brain tells you to adhere to the agreement as long as the long-term payoff of doing so is bigger than the long-term payoff of cheating. That is, you will follow the agreement as long as

$$\frac{2}{1+\delta} \geq 3 + \frac{1}{1+\delta}.$$

If we rearrange this, we see that we will follow the agreement if $\delta \geq \frac{1}{2}$ for this game.[5] This value of delta is determined by the particular payoffs of the game. If I were to change the numbers in the game matrix, then delta will change—one half is not some magic number.

The interpretation of this value is that, as long as tomorrow is at least half as important to me as today is, I will adhere to the agreement. This makes perfect sense—since my motive to adhere to the contract is driven by my fear of future penalties. Thus, the more I value the future, the more I fear those forthcoming penalties, and the less I am willing to sacrifice tomorrow's payoff for one-time glory today.

---

[5] Technically, you are indifferent between adhering to the agreement and cheating if $\delta = \frac{1}{2}$, but I assume that your indifference results in honest play. Nothing changes if we assume the opposite response to your indifference.

Application to Immigration Decisions

The material in the previous two sections seemingly has little to do with immigration, in part because it is a little on the abstract side compared to some things we have seen in other chapters. However, I don't want you to forget what game theory tells us—it shows us how two parties interact. More specifically, the idea of cooperative equilibria helps us understand when a contract or an agreement will be followed and when one or more of the parties will violate the agreement.

To apply these ideas to immigration, we need only define who the parties are who are playing the "game" and eventually describe what the contract or agreement is between them. The government is clearly one of the participants, and a randomly selected immigrant is the other. I say "randomly selected" because I want to pretend that a large group of immigrants all making one decision is the same as one immigrant making repeated decisions over time. This way we can use our understanding of repeated games to analyze immigration decisions.

Let's start with a simple game where a potential immigrant is deciding whether to migrate legally or illegally, and the government is deciding how much money to spend enforcing immigration laws. So the actions available to the immigrant are "legal" or "illegal," and the government has either "lax" or "strict" as possible moves. Let's simplify and specify somewhat, and assume that there 100 people thinking of migrating. If the immigrant move is "legal," then 80/100 will try to enter legally, and 20/100 will try to enter illegally. Symmetrically, if the move is "illegal," then 20/100 will try to enter legally, and 80/100 will try to do so illegally. Regardless of the move made by immigrants, only 50 people are admitted legally due to paperwork constraints. As for the government's moves, a lax policy will capture up to 12 illegal immigrants, while the strict version will capture nearly four times as many—up to 45 illegal immigrants.

There is no agreement yet. The payoffs to each party are going to have special meaning in this example. For the immigrant, the payoff number is going to represent the percentage of immigrants who wanted to migrate and did so. For example, a payoff of 65 implies that 65% of people interested in moving actually migrated. For the government, the payoff number is going to represent the percentage of illegal immigrants captured. Presumably, the government would like this number to be as large as possible. With these things in mind, the normal form of this game might look something like this:

		Government	
		lax	strict
Immigrant	legal	(58, 60)	(50, 100)
	illegal	(88, 15)	(55, 56 ¼)

Let's carefully pick apart the payoffs shown in the game above.

1. Moves "legal" and "lax" results in the ordered pair (58, 60). Of the 100 people interested in migrating, 80 take the time to fill out paperwork. Of these 80, only 50 are admitted thanks to constraints within the government. In addition to those legally admitted, 20 people migrate illegally, but only 12 of these are caught thanks to the lax policy by the government. Thus, the total number of people successful in migrating is 50 legal and 8 illegal for a total of 58. The government here has chosen to employ a lax policy of enforcing illegal migration, but they got lucky—the majority of immigrants chose to migrate legally, so the number of illegal immigrants is moderate. Of the 20 who entered the country illegally, the government catches 12, giving them a score of 12/20 = 60 (the payoffs are percentages!).

2. "legal" and "strict" results in payoffs of (50, 100). The legal move by immigrants means 80 apply and 50 get in legally. As before, 20 people try entering illegally, but the government has stepped up their policy, so that all 20 get caught (recall, the government can catch up to 45 people if they play "strict"). The net for immigrants is thus 50 (all legal), and the government hit 100%.

3. "illegal" and "lax" results in payoffs of (88, 15). Since immigrants played "illegal," only 20/100 people went through legal channels, and since up to 50 are admitted, all 20 get in. Further, 80/100 people decided to forgo the paperwork, and entered the country illegally. Most of these got lucky because the government had decided to be lax on illegal immigration, so they catch only 12 of the 80, giving us a 15% capture rate (12/80 = 15%). Immigrants have 20 legal and 68 illegal entrants, for a total of 88.

4. "illegal" and "strict" results in payoffs of (55, 56.25). As before, all 20 legal applicants are admitted. But the government's strict policy captures up to 45 illegal immigrants. Since 80 try to enter illegally with this strategy, the government catches 45/80 = 56.25%. This means that there are 20 legal and 35 illegal immigrants, for a total of 55.

Now, how should each party play this game? From the average immigrant's point of view, "illegal" is better than "legal" if the government is lax (88 instead of 58). Likewise, moving "illegal" is better than "legal" if the government is strict (55 instead of 50). Thus, playing "illegal" is always better, regardless of the government's move—so immigrants should play "illegal" always. From the government's point of view, "strict" is better than "lax" if immigrants play "legal" (100 versus 60). Further, "strict" is better than "lax" if immigrants play "illegal" (56¼ instead of 15). Thus, the government sees that "strict" is always their best move—no matter what immigrants do. So, it follows that the average immigrant will always play "illegal," the government will always play "strict," and we will always end up in the lower right corner with payoffs of (55, 56¼).

Is this the best that the two parties can do? As we saw in the prisoners' dilemma example at the end of the previous section, it may be possible for the two players to enter an agreement that is mutually beneficial. Here, the agreement between the government and the immigrant may seem a little peculiar: the immigrant agrees to not immigrate illegally, and in return the government agrees to make only a minimal effort and investment into enforcing immigration laws. Specifically, the immigrants have to promise play "legal" and the government will promise to play "lax." Doing so will allow us to move to the upper left corner, increasing payoffs to both parties to (58, 60). However, just as before, if either side reneges on this agreement, the other player will penalize them by switching strategies and the game will forever end up at the less attractive (55, 56¼). Notice that the cooperative equilibrium is better for both parties—there are more immigrants successful in migrating (58 instead of 55), the government has a higher success rate in capturing illegal immigrants (60% instead of 56¼%), and there are fewer illegal immigrants (8 instead of 35).[6]

So, according to this example, a cooperative equilibrium can in fact be reached between the government and immigrants that results in more immigrants being admitted, fewer illegal immigrants, and less expenditure by the government on enforcement (lax is cheaper than strict). So why does the United States spend so much time on enforcement efforts, and why is such a large percentage of the immigrant population illegal? It's possible you support the claim that one of the two parties has historically violated what would have been an agreement (maybe the agreement was implicit at the time). Perhaps immigrants played "illegal" too often, and the government is responding by playing "strict."

Another possible explanation has to do with the delicacy of constructing an example like this. It was actually kind of tricky to pick payoffs, capture rates, and all of the other variables in such a way that the example supported the point I was trying to make (this is partly why the numbers are kind of weird—whole numbers would have been nice). This implies that the details of this game are too artificial, which means the cooperative equilibrium may not really exist. It's possible no such agreement could be mutually beneficial.

A third, and perhaps more straightforward, explanation is interestingly evident from the particular numbers used for this example, albeit for coincidental reasons. It's possible, or even likely, that the difference in payoffs between the cooperative equilibrium and the non-cooperative equilibrium is too small to justify the cost of designing the contract. Essentially, if payoffs under cooperation are only slightly higher, why bother with the contract? Contracts aren't free to design or enforce, and this one would be particularly expensive due to the vast number of potential immigrants.

Finally, it's possible that a contract of this nature can't be developed due to the diverse and heterogeneous group of potential immigrants. As we have seen, there is an abundance of data that support the claim that immigrants are a mixed group of

---

6   Remember, in one case 20 tried and 12 were caught for a total of 8. In the other case 80 tried and 45 were caught for a total of 35.

people. Skills vary, opportunity cost of migration varies, travel costs vary, preferences are not uniform—all of which make a single contract unlikely. Perhaps my risk aversion is different from yours. If so, then I might think the contract is a good idea, and you may say "why bother ... let's just risk it." This disagreement means the contract won't be effective, and we are doomed to live at the inferior equilibrium.

Chapter 10

Immigration Around the World

The primary focus of much of this text has been immigration to the United States. Although many of the tools studied and arguments made can be used in other settings, we find ourselves coming back to the case of the United States for several reasons. The first is that we are here, and our economic analysis of immigration issues obviously revolves around things we know and see. Second is the fact that the United States has a lot of immigration—we essentially founded our country on the principle that immigrants add to the stew in flavorful ways. (The term "melting pot" comes to mind.) Finally, since we have a developed nation and a typically functioning government, we have access to an abundance of data. The lack of data proves to be a very troublesome obstacle to people interested in measuring these effects in certain parts of the world.

That said, immigration is a huge part of many economies around the world. This has been the case for hundreds and hundreds of years—since the Portuguese were sailing around the world and Vikings were visiting North America. The article below gives some anecdotal evidence of the importance of immigration to countries around the world (WSJ, 2/6/2012).

Seeking Safeguards for Unskilled Workers Abroad

By Eric Bellman
Wall Street Journal, February 6, 2012

Jakarta—Indonesia, the Philippines and other developing countries are demanding more rights and higher wages worldwide for their legions of unskilled laborers—a trend that could shake up global labor markets.

The most recent battles have centered on maids, whose ranks have swelled in recent years in rich nations in the Middle East, Asia and elsewhere. The fight has implications beyond house cleaners and nannies. Advocates are hoping the push for more rights for domestic servants will spread to other unskilled migrants, as some

---

countries grow increasingly reliant on imported cheap labor to baby-sit for their children, staff their factories and build their skyscrapers.

The millions who go abroad to take jobs as domestic workers—mostly women employed as maids, but also including such traditionally male jobs as gardeners and cooks—are a crucial source of foreign currency back home, and are emerging as an important vote bank.

The poorer nations that supply the labor are now insisting their citizens receive better protection, fair pay, equal treatment under local laws and weekly days off.

The United Nations' International Labor Organization is helping propel the campaign. Last year, it pushed through an international convention to protect domestic workers around the globe that outlines some basic rights, such as fixed working hours and weekly holidays.

The Philippines—one of the world's biggest exporters of labor in general, with close to eight million citizens working abroad at any given time—recently blacklisted more than 40 countries for not having proper labor safeguards. The Philippines recently got Saudi Arabia to agree to impose minimum salaries and other benefits. Filipino maids recently won a landmark case in Hong Kong, granting full-time residency to those who have been living there at least a decade.

"This can be traced from a history of abuse that many of our overseas workers are encountering," said Rosalinda Baldoz, the Philippines' secretary of labor and employment. "We want more transparency in terms and conditions."

Indonesia also has clashed with Saudi Arabia. Indonesian authorities last year blocked the country's domestic workers from going to the kingdom, following reports of rape and torture of its citizens working in private homes, along with the more common complaints of contract violations. In one case, a maid was beheaded, without warning, after being found guilty of the murder of her employer, according to Indonesian officials, who say they believe it may have been a matter of self-defense.

Saudi Arabian authorities didn't respond to requests to comment.

Cambodia, after reports of abuse, has stopped its domestic workers from going to Malaysia.

In January, Indonesia's Manpower and Transmigration Minister Muhaimin Iskandar threatened to block all Indonesian maids from taking jobs overseas in the next five years if more progress isn't made. The government also wants better monitoring of brokers and hiring households.

"Host countries need to start recognizing normal rights, such as to set working hours, leave and minimum wages," said Jumhur Hidayat, an adviser to Indonesia's president on overseas worker issues.

Malaysian authorities said they are taking steps to ensure the rights of Indonesian maids will be respected, and that a new accord with the Indonesian government—which also guarantees workers' rights to hold on to their own passports, rather than have them held by employer or their agency—will apply to maids from March.

In home countries, politicians are starting to acknowledge the potential clout of the millions of maids and their families as an important block of constituents. Some countries, including India and the Philippines, are looking for ways to make it easier for their overseas workers to vote in elections.

Meanwhile, remittances from overseas workers to developing countries have quadrupled in the past 11 years, according to the World Bank, to more than $350 billion. In the Philippines, remittances are equal to nearly 11% of its gross domestic product.

Labor economists say they expect tensions to increase as more workers look overseas for opportunities.

The number of migrant domestic workers has jumped in the past decade. Lower airfares, improved communications and the spread of the Internet have made it easier to travel and to share information about job opportunities.

The increased global connectivity also has spread horror stories faster, raising the awareness of the need for more protection for overseas workers.

Some labor-importing countries are pushing back on the new demands. Malaysians have started looking for domestic help from other sources, such as Vietnam. Singapore has tightened restrictions on all types of immigration.

Saudi Arabia last year said it would stop accepting maids from Indonesia and the Philippines, even as Indonesia banned its workers from going there. Riyadh is in the middle of a drive to reduce the number of foreigners working in the country by hiring Saudis, though the move is mostly fueled by fears that low youth employment fed the uprisings in neighboring Mideast countries.

—*Yayu Yuniar and Celine Fernandez contributed to this article.*

Two Special Cases

There are two countries that deserve special attention concerning immigration outside of the United States. The first is Germany, the second is Japan. These two countries actually share some striking similarities. For example, both countries have relatively homogeneous populations, at least superficially. However, the differences between the two countries are what make them an interesting pair for study, as we will see. In the end, however, both countries face the same types of questions that we face in the United States: who will migrate, what will they do to our economy, and what should our immigration policy look like?

Germany[1]

In the past decade, immigration issues have become popular in Europe as the EU tries to push toward consistency in immigration policy for member nations. For example, a couple of 2005 reports released by the Commission of the European Communities titled *Green Paper: On an EU Approach to Managing Economic Migration* and *Policy Plan on Legal Migration* have tried to fuel discussion and foster development of consistent policies concerning migration for migrants within the EU and for those arriving from non-member countries.

One of the primary concerns for Germany is the loss of high-skill labor. As we have seen in previous sections, the United States has benefited historically from the flight of skill from European nations, particularly from Germany. Similarly, the UK, Canada, and Australia have been recipients of skilled immigrant labor from Germany. As we will see, maintaining a supply of skilled labor is a priority for Germany, and it follows that they should try to cater an immigration policy that supports this goal.

There are a few things that we may have to remind ourselves of as we proceed through the German case of immigration. The first is that Germany has a lot of neighbors—eight other countries share a border with Germany. Second, unlike most Americans, Europeans tend to be proficient in several languages, thanks to the proximity of neighboring countries. (If people in Indiana spoke a different language than the people in Illinois, I assure you more Chicagoans would be bilingual.) This skill (yes, this counts as a skill—as in "skilled worker"—it's another form of human capital!) makes migration much easier. If a job opens in Germany, a Swiss worker could start tomorrow without any concern for language barriers.

German Immigration History

In the post-WWII era, a rebuilding Germany relied heavily on guest workers from places like Spain, Greece, Turkey, Morocco, Portugal, and Tunisia, with whom they shared an agreement allowing for recruitment of workers. However, declining economic climate led to a ban of recruitment in 1966. The ban lapsed for a while after a new agreement with Yugoslavia in 1968, but resumed in 1973 in light of the negative economic impact caused by the oil crisis. During this period, the foreign population of Germany doubled.

In 1991, Germany passed the Federal Aliens Act that took steps to limit the number of immigrants, with the notable exception of Jewish immigrants from former Soviet

---

[1]   This section relies heavily on Zimmermann, Klaus, H. Bonin, R. Fahr, and H. Hinte, "Immigration Policy and the Labor Market: The German Experience and Lessons for Europe." Springer (2007).

territories. Interestingly, 1992 brought a quota system specifically designed for immigrants of German ethnicity. In 1996, language proficiency tests were introduced, and restrictions on place of residence were imposed on people entering the country. (These residency restrictions were designed to prevent the establishment of ethnic ghettos by requiring immigrants to live at prescribed locations for a period of time in order to be eligible for social welfare and transfer payments.) Naturalization takes eight years, and citizenship is granted to children whose parents are naturalized or were born in Germany (only one parent satisfying this will suffice).

In 2000, the Federal Government Independent Commission on Immigration was appointed to develop recommendations for the modification of Germany's immigration policies, many of which were adopted in 2001. This act allowed for the selection of immigrants via a point system, as well as the use of quotas to limit the total number of immigrants. Modifications occurred in 2002 (the original act was declared void by the Federal Constitutional Court) and 2004, when a weaker version was finally adopted.

A graphical summary of how these immigration policies affected the number of German immigrants is shown in Figure 10.1 below.[2]

Figure 10.1

Gross and net migration in Germany (1955–2004)

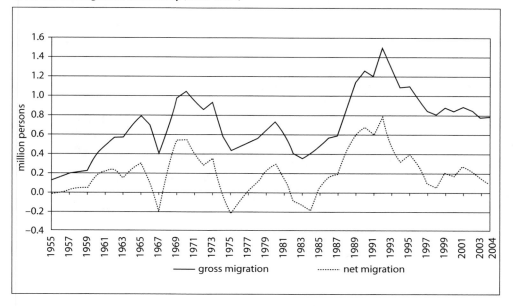

[2]   Zimmerman, p. 17

Figure 10.2

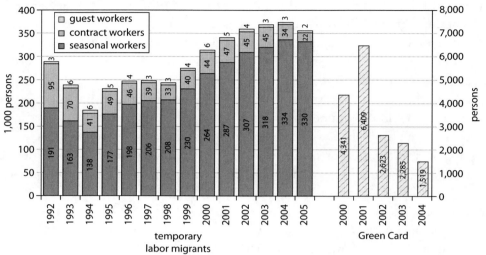

Temporary labor migration from non-EU countries

Notes: Other special forms of temporary immigration and work permit (specialized personnel of German-foreign corporations, artists, scientists, au-pairs, etc.) not included. Numbers in thousands based on addition of the three forms of labor migration referred to above.

Source: Federal Office for Migration and Refugees (BAMF), Migrationsbericht 2005.

Since a large percentage of German immigration has historically involved recruited workers and temporary or seasonal workers designed to fill shortages in Germany's labor force, duration of stay may be brief for immigrants. (We know that the southern United States experiences a lot of short-term visitors from Mexico.) However, in the opposite direction, Germany did experience a period during which family reunification was popular, particularly during the second half of the 1970s decade after the ban on worker recruitment. Figure 10.2 shows some data concerning temporary worker immigration, and Figure 10.3 examines duration of stay.[3]

---

[3]   Zimmerman, p. 28 and p. 20

Figure 10.3

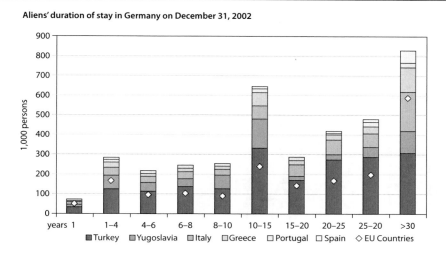

Aliens' duration of stay in Germany on December 31, 2002

As we discussed at length in previous sections, the positive impact of immigration relies intimately on the fact that they work after arriving. For Germany, early immigration was primarily recruited workers. However, after the ban, we see that the number of non-working immigrants has increased tremendously, as shown in Figure 10.4 below.[4]

Figure 10.4

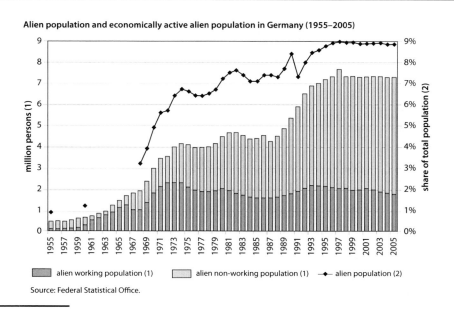

Alien population and economically active alien population in Germany (1955–2005)

Source: Federal Statistical Office.

<hr />

[4] Zimmerman, p. 27

Figure 10.5

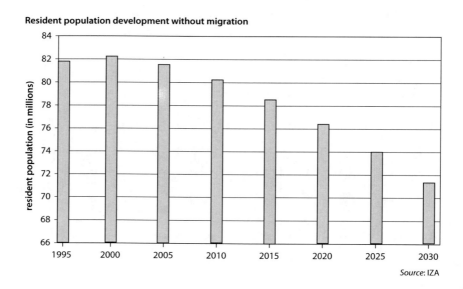

Resident population development without migration

Source: IZA

The Disappearing German Population and the Future of German Immigration

The German Institute for the Study of Labor (abbreviated IZA), has made some projections concerning the stability of the population of Germany, as well as the impact of an aging German population on the size of the labor force. As it turns out immigration may serve as necessary injection of manpower for a dwindling labor supply, as the data below show.[5] The first figure, Figure 10.5, shows the projected contraction of the population in the absence of immigration. As you can see, a decline of approximately 10% is expected over the next two decades.

However, population size alone does not necessarily have measurable impacts on economic performance. In fact, a small population can foster a robust economy, as long as the portion of working-age people is sufficient. Unfortunately, we see a similar declining trend in the number of working-age people in Germany, even with under several potential immigration cases, as Figure 10.6 illustrates.

---

[5] Zimmerman, p. 91 and p. 31

Figure 10.6

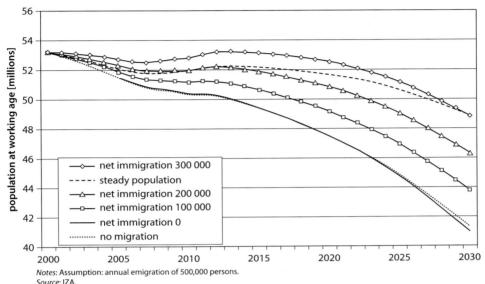

Population at working age (18–64 years old), subject to different migration balances, 2000–2030

Notes: Assumption: annual emigration of 500,000 persons.
Source: IZA.

It has been estimated that, by 2030, Germany would need to import nearly one million immigrant workers to keep the size of the labor force constant. This forecast is made under the assumption that neither emigration rates nor labor participation rates by natives change over time. Germany nets less than one quarter of this number currently. (Keep in mind, unlike in the United States, emigration is a major concern for Germany. In fact, as Figure 10.1 showed, Germany loses almost as many people as it gains each year. Clearly, with these trends, Germany needs to design an immigration policy that can effectively address a potential shrinking of both population and labor force.

Unfortunately for Germany, they seem to be intent on piecing together a policy based on systems already in use in the United States, Canada, New Zealand, and Australia. As we have seen, all of these countries, with the exception of the United States, employ some sort of point system to filter the quality of immigrants entering the country. However, it is unclear if these countries face the same demographic issues that Germany sees on the horizon. I suspect that, if the data here are reliable, Germany's best bet for an immigration policy is to open the floodgates. Of course, as we know well, this doesn't come without costs.

Table 10.1

The number of permanent residence permissions and naturalization permissions

Year	Permanent residence permission								Naturalisation permission				
	Total	Chinese	Filipino	Koreans	Brazilians	Peruvian	Others	Rejects	Total	Koreans	Chinese	Others	Rejects
1990	5,663	1,028	142	3,666	32	5	790	260	6,794	5,216	1,349	229	274
1991	5,469	1,236	227	2,963	35	4	1,004	240	7,788	5,665	1,818	305	223
1992	4,078	1,325	313	1,238	39	11	1,152	474	9,363	7,244	1,794	325	162
1993	3,848	1067	387	1,247	37	17	1,098	412	10,452	7,697	2,244	511	126
1994	6,846	2,123	1,024	2,025	111	29	1,534	647	11,146	8,244	2,478	424	146
1995	5,932	1,901	1,112	1,376	105	54	1,384	366	14,104	10,327	3,184	593	93
1996	9,556	2,958	1,783	1,935	359	474	2,047	606	14,495	9,856	3,976	621	97
1997	11,583	3,372	2,088	1,937	814	1,133	2,239	645	15,061	9,678	4,729	654	90
1998	12,934	3,837	2,495	2,091	957	1,304	2,250	1,529	14,779	9,561	4,637	581	108
1999	19,731	6,514	3,973	2,782	1,689	1,497	3,276	2,662	16,120	10,059	5,335	726	202
2000	30,475	10,593	5,467	3,454	3,762	2,323	4,876	2,471	15,812	9,842	5,245	725	215

Japan[6]

Japan has a very long history of island-nation mentality. They are isolated from their neighbors geographically, and as a result, have maintained a demographic seemingly free of outsiders. The popular attitude about outsiders supports this homogeneity. Immigration is such a foreign concept to most Japanese natives (the pun was definitely intended…) that most have probably never considered the pros and cons of importing workers. However, as we saw in the case of Germany, Japan is faced with an aging population and a low birth rate. The result is a potential labor shortage for which immigration presents an attractive solution. As a result, there has been much recent debate concerning Japanese immigration policy.

Historically, Japan's immigration policy has been incredibly strict, starting with what is known as the "isolation period" from 1639 to 1853. The following 90 years until WWII represent the only period of active migration, both to and from Japan. However, since WWII, Japan has had a very strict policy of limiting admissions, even despite their profound economic growth during the post-war period. For example, a twenty-year residency requirement was required for permanent resident status. (Ironic, I think, that after 20 years you would finally be considered a "permanent" resident.

---

[6]   Much of the data in this section have come from the Statistics Bureau, part of the Ministry of Internal Affairs and Communications.

Table 10.2

Foreign workers in Japan by status of residence, 1996–2000

Status of residence	1996	1997	1998	1999	2000
Entertainer	20,103	22,185	28,871	32,297	53,847
Specialist in humanities or international service	27,377	29,941	31,285	31,766	34,739
Engineer	11,052	12,874	15,242	15,668	16,531
Skilled labor	8,767	9,608	10,048	10,459	11,349
Intra-company transferee	5,941	6,372	6,599	7,377	8,657
Instructor	7,514	7,769	7,941	8,079	8,375
Professor	4,573	5,086	5,374	5,879	6,744
Investor and business manager	5,014	5,055	5,112	5,440	5,694
Religious activities	5,010	5,061	4,910	4,962	4,976
Researcher	2,019	2,462	2,762	2,896	2,934
Artist	272	276	309	351	363
Journalist	454	420	373	361	349
Legal and accounting service	65	58	59	77	95
Medical service	140	131	111	114	95

This has recently been shortened, but as the table below shows, the total number of permissions is relatively low. (For reference, Japan is about half the size of the United States in terms of population and GDP.)

The trend of isolationism and exclusionary policy is further evident if we consider the number of foreign workers, as Table 10.2 illustrates.

It should be noted that the rarity of foreign workers is not entirely due to the lack of willingness to migrate to Japan for work. Instead, it seems clear that Japan's immigration policy is largely responsible for the small immigrant workforce. For example, as the following data show, the number of illegal workers is quite large when taken as a percent of total immigrant workers. It turns out that the number of deported illegal immigrants would comprise approximately one third of the total legal immigrant labor force.

Table 10.3

Number of deported illegal workers by citizenship 1996–2000

Citizenship	1996	1997	1998	1999	2000	%
South Korea	11,444	10,346	9,360	13,164	11,336	25.7
China (Mainland)	7,403	7,810	7,224	8,278	8,132	18.4
(Taiwan)	437	557	429	466	492	1.1
(Hong Kong etc.)	82	112	53	60	36	0.1
The Philippines	5,646	5,067	5,631	6,672	7,420	16.8
Thailand	5,561	4,483	3,604	3,926	3,902	8.8
Iran	3,180	2,225	2,219	1,639	1,598	3.6
Peru	4,034	1,694	1,746	1,459	1,458	3.3
Malaysia	2,214	1,579	1,350	1,429	1,288	2.9
Pakistan	1,418	1,152	1,255	1,314	1,217	2.8
Indonesia	817	957	1,210	1,220	1,090	2.4
Bangladesh	926	930	1,067	1,082	1,073	2.4
Others	4,623	4,692	5,387	5,549	5,148	11.5
Total	47,785	41,604	40,535	46,258	44,190	100.0

Recall that in the United States, apprehensions of illegal immigrants result in over one million deportations and voluntary departures each year. In contrast, Japan sees only 40,000. Clearly the importance of immigration in Japan is insignificant compared to the United States.

Japan's Grim Immigrant-less Future

Consider figures 10.7 to 10.9. As you can see, the population growth rate in Japan has slowed to a crawl, and as a result the overall population size as remained largely unchanged (especially in percent terms) for several years. Figure 10.9 shows what is called a "pyramid" graph of the population, which shows the age group by gender. What would a pyramid graph look like for a country poised for economic growth?

If the 2050 projection is accurate, nearly 40% of the Japanese population will be retired. If we add to this the percent of the population that is too young to work, we are near 50%. Factor in labor participation rates and we see that the working 25% of

Figure 10.7

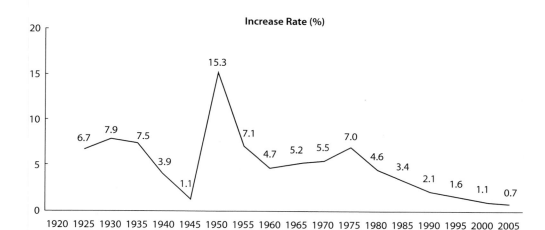

the population will be responsible for supporting the out-of-work 75% of the nation. This is not a bright forecast for the third largest economy in the world.

I'm sure you've heard a similar-sounding concern about the United States, in that our population is getting older. This is part of the concern about the Social Security system in the coming decades as the entire baby boom population reaches retirement. However, as the figure below shows, Japan appears to be in far bigger trouble than the United States.

Figure 10.8

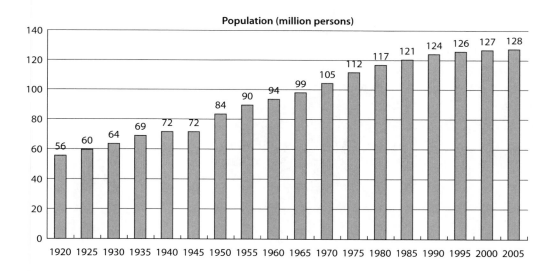

Figure 10.9

Changes in the Population Pyramid

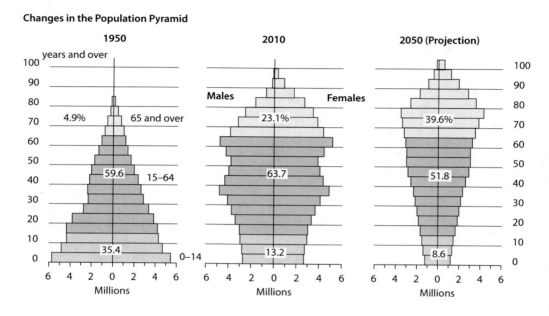

It should be noted that Japan is not unaware of these problems. In fact, a report from the Population Division of the Department of Economic and Social Affairs of the United Nations titled *Replacement Migration: Is It a Solution to Declining and Aging Populations?* discussed these issues. This report concluded that, in order to stabilize their population at the 1995 level, Japan would need to import 33.5 million immigrants between now and 2050. This averages to nearly three quarters of a million immigrants annually.

It may be hard for a typical resident of the United States to understand this situation, since we see an abundance of immigration on a regular basis. However, the resistance to immigration by Japanese culture seems to be almost genetic. I recently attended a seminar on the topic of immigration in Japan where several Japanese economists presented papers outlining their suggested solutions to the inevitable issues caused by Japan's shrinking population. Several of these papers suggested completely implausible or inferior alternatives to immigration, such as encouraging female labor-force participation (… but females are aging too …) or outsourcing to solve labor-shortage issues (and in turn you will outsource the immigration surplus we found earlier).

Figure 10.10

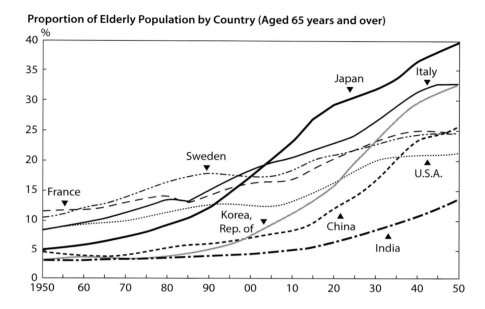

Proportion of Elderly Population by Country (Aged 65 years and over)

Perhaps the comparison of the Japanese view of immigration juxtaposed on the American view is a good way to conclude this text for now, because it really highlights how difficult the issue of immigration is. It seems that there is no right answer to questions like how much immigration is optimal, what kinds of immigrants are optimal, and what policy works the best. Unfortunately, these are questions that need to be answered at some point.

Credits

Miriam Jordan, "Green-Card Lottery Record," *The Wall Street Journal*. Copyright © 2010 by Dow Jones & Company, Inc. Reprinted with permission.

Miriam Jordan, "Soldier Finds Minefield on Road to Citizenship," *The Wall Street Journal*. Copyright © 2010 by Dow Jones & Company, Inc. Reprinted with permission.

Miriam Jordan, "Policing Illegal Hires Puts Some Employers in a Bind," *The Wall Street Journal*. Copyright © 2010 by Dow Jones & Company, Inc. Reprinted with permission.

Miriam Jordan, "With Jobs on the U.S. Scarce, Illegal Immigration Slides," *The Wall Street Journal*. Copyright © 2010 by Dow Jones & Company, Inc. Reprinted with permission.

Guy Chazan, "Tough Irish Economy Turns Migration Influx to Exodus," *The Wall Street Journal*. Copyright © 2011 by Dow Jones & Company, Inc. Reprinted with permission.

Keith Johnson, "Homeland Security Scraps Border Fence," *The Wall Street Journal*. Copyright © 2011 by Dow Jones & Company, Inc. Reprinted with permission.

Lauren Etter, "Border Fight Creeps North," *The Wall Street Journal*. Copyright © 2010 by Dow Jones & Company, Inc. Reprinted with permission.

Stu Woo, "Immigrants Win on College Fees," *The Wall Street Journal*. Copyright © 2010 by Dow Jones & Company, Inc. Reprinted with permission.

Ana Campoy, "Deportation Program Grows," *The Wall Street Journal*. Copyright © 2010 by Dow Jones & Company, Inc. Reprinted with permission.

Emma Lazarus, "The New Colossus," *The Statue of Liberty*. Copyright in the Public Domain.

Images and Tables

Green card image, p. 37. Source: www.green-card.com/images/main/GreenCard-800x513.jpg.

Table 8.3, p. 151. Source: IZA.

Gross and Net Migration in Germany, 1955–2004 (Figure 10.1, p .175). Source: Federal Statistical Office.

Temporary Labor Migration from Non-EU Countries (Figure 10.2, p. 176). Source: Federal Office for Migration and Refugees (BAMF), Migrationsbericht 2005.

Aliens' Duration of Stay in Germany on December 31, 2002 (Figure 10.3, p. 177). Source: Federal Statistical Office.

Alien Population and Economically Active Alien Population in Germany, 1955–2005 (Figure 10.4, p. 177). Source: Federal Statistical Office.

Resident Population Development Without Migration (Figure 10.5, p. 178). Source: IZA.

The Number of Permanent Residence Permissions and Naturalization Permissions (Table 10.1, p. 180). Source: Ministry of Justice. Cleared via Crown Copyright's Open Government License.

Foreign Workers in Japan by Status of Residence, 1996–2000 (Table 10.2, p. 181). Source: Ministry of Justice. Cleared via Crown Copyright's Open Government License.

Number of Deported Illegal Workers by Citizenship, 1996–2000 (Table 10.3, p. 182). Source: Ministry of Justice. Cleared via Crown Copyright's Open Government License.

Changes in the Population Pyramid (Figure 10.9, p. 184). Source: Statistics Bureau, MIC.

Proportion of Elderly Population by Country, Aged 65 Years and Over (Figure 10.10, p. 185). Source: Statistics Bureau, MIC.